MORE MAKING OUT IN KOREAN

Revised Edition Expanded

by **Ghi-woon Seo**
Revised by **Laura Kingdon and Chris Backe**

TUTTLE Publishing

Tokyo | Rutland, Vermont | Singapore

ABOUT TUTTLE
"Books to Span the East and West"

Our core mission at Tuttle Publishing is to create books which bring people together one page at a time. Tuttle was founded in 1832 in the small New England town of Rutland, Vermont (USA). Our fundamental values remain as strong today as they were then—to publish best-in-class books informing the English-speaking world about the countries and peoples of Asia. The world has become a smaller place today and Asia's economic, cultural and political influence has expanded, yet the need for meaningful dialogue and information about this diverse region has never been greater. Since 1948, Tuttle has been a leader in publishing books on the cultures, arts, cuisines, languages and literatures of Asia. Our authors and photographers have won numerous awards and Tuttle has published thousands of books on subjects ranging from martial arts to paper crafts. We welcome you to explore the wealth of information available on Asia at **www.tuttlepublishing.com**.

Published by Tuttle Publishing, an imprint of Periplus Editions (HK) Ltd.

www.tuttlepublishing.com

Copyright © 2008, 2015 Periplus Editions (HK) Ltd.
Illustrations by Dami Lee
All rights reserved.

ISBN 978-0-8048-4356-0

20 19 18 17
6 5 4 3 2   1703RR

Printed in China

Distributed by:

North America, Latin America & Europe
Tuttle Publishing
364 Innovation Drive, North Clarendon
VT 05759-9436, USA
Tel: 1 (802) 773 8930 | Fax: 1 (802) 773 6993
info@tuttlepublishing.com
www.tuttlepublishing.com

Japan
Tuttle Publishing
Yaekari Building 3F, 5-4-12 Osaki, Shinagawa-ku,
Tokyo 141-0032, Japan
Tel: (81) 3 5437 0171 | Fax: (81) 3 5437 0755
sales@tuttle.co.jp
www.tuttle.co.jp

Asia Pacific
Berkeley Books Pte. Ltd.
61 Tai Seng Avenue #02-12, Singapore 534167
Tel: (65) 6280-1330 | Fax: (65) 6280-6290
inquiries@periplus.com.sg
www.periplus.com

TUTTLE PUBLISHING® is a registered trademark of Tuttle Publishing,
a division of Periplus Editions (HK) Ltd.

Contents

Introduction

Korean is considered one of the most difficult languages for Western people to learn. It reflects a different word order, alphabet (Hangeul) and culture.

If you go to a bookstore and browse the books with titles starting "Learn Korean," chances are you're gonna find yourself murmuring, "Is it an alphabet?" "It looks like pictures to me" (or even "It's all Greek to me"), "I don't think I can learn Korean," and so on.

Why don't you start with interesting, easy, familiar topics first? Imagine you are going to be visiting Korea in a week, and you don't know any Korean words or expressions yet. You need a handy but useful book, so that you can speak Korean from the first moment you land at Seoul's Incheon International Airport.

Well then, *More Making Out in Korean* is the book for you! Just like you would read a magazine, you can take it easy, relax, and skim through this book.

Korean has various speech styles according to the speaker's age, social status, intimacy and so forth. While the book *Making Out in Korean* focuses on "intimate speech level," the expressions in this book are based on normal speech style, which can be used with anyone from a total stranger to an intimate friend without making him / her embarrassed. Therefore, you can use the expressions without worrying that you might be considered rude. This book also includes current slang used by Korean young people, especially on the Internet.

Now, let's hit the road!

One Thing You Should Keep In Mind

In English, calling the person in front of you "You" is not inappropriate ("You are so beautiful," "Do you like it?" and so on). However, in Korean it's different. You have to be very careful when you call a Korean **Neo** (*nuh*) or **Dangsin** (*dahngshin*), meaning "you." Instead, it is more appropriate (1) to omit "you" or (2) to use his / her name followed by **-ssi**, a suffix used when addressing a person (for example, **John-ssi**, **Cheolsu-ssi**). Here is an example of each of these ways to avoid "you":

(1)

John, did [you] see it? (Did [you] see it?)
(to a person you don't know)

Geugeo bwasseoyo?
Geuguh bwassuh-yo?
그거 봤어요?

(2)

Did you see it? (John, did [you] see it?)
(to John)

John-ssi, geugeo bwasseoyo? (to John)
John-sshee, geuguh bwahssuh-yo?
잔씨, 그거 봤어요?

For this reason—the importance in Korean of not using "you" rudely—this book mostly uses **-ssi** instead of using **neo** or **dangsin**.

BASIC GRAMMAR

Korean sentences use a different word order than the Subject-Verb-Object you are used to in English. Korean uses Subject-Object-Verb. The verbs are very important in Korean, and so they have the prime position as the "final word" of a sentence.

I am going to school.   **Hakkyoe gayo.**
                              (Statement)
                              Hahk-kkyo-ay gahyo.
                              학교에 가요.

Literally means "School to go."

Verbs are so important in Korean, in fact, that—just as long as you can still gather the meaning from the context—you can omit any other element of the sentence, except the verb. So a verb alone can form a complete sentence.

Are you going?   **Gayo?** (Question)
                      Gahyo?
                      가요?

Literally means "Go?"

As in many languages, one sentence can actually convey several different things—a command or a question for example—simply based on the context and on your tone of voice:

Let's go to school.   Hakkyoe gayo.
                                 (Suggestion)
                                 Hahk-kkyo-ay gahyo.
                                 학교에 가요.

Literally means "School to go."

Going to school!   Hakkyoe gayo!
  (You must be   (Exclamation)
  joking!)   *Hahk-kkyo-ay gahyo!*
                                 학교에 가요!

Literally means "School to go."

You can also do a lot in Korean just by changing the way your verbs end. The examples above all show a very common and versatile verb ending, but you can add all kinds of further nuances by using different endings with different meanings. In our example sentence here, the verb is "to go," or 가다 (*ga-da*) in Korean, and you can change that verb 가다 (*ga-da*) to give your sentence different meanings. For example:

Are you going to school?   Hakkyoe ganayo?
(question)   *Hahk-kyoh-ay gah-nah-yo?*
                                 학교에 가나요?

Go to school.   Hakkyoe gashipshio.
                                   (extremely formal and
                                   polite)
                                 *Hahk-kyoh-ay gah-ship-
                                   shee-oh.*
                                 학교에 가십시오.

You're going to school!	Hakkyoe ganeyo! (exclamation) *Hahk-kyoh-ay gah-nay-yo!* 학교에 가네요!

READING KOREAN, USING THE ENGLISH ALPHABET

In this book, the upper line on the right of the page shows the Romanized version of the phrase. Romanizing is a system of writing Korean using the letters you're used to in English. It follows Korea's official Romanization system. The letters used in this Romanization system must be pronounced in a specific way.

Because it can be difficult for English speakers to read Romanized Korean correctly, we've also supplied a phonetic guide, in italics beneath it. This is designed to reflect the closest English equivalent to each Korean sound.

Each phrase is also shown in Korean script. So if you have a hard time making yourself understood, you can show the book to the person you're speaking with, and they'll be able to read what you're trying to say.

SIMPLE CONSONANTS

There are two kinds of consonants in Korean. The simple consonants are pronounced as in English.

ㄱ **g, k**	ㄴ **n**	ㄷ **d, t**	ㄹ **r, l**	ㅁ **m**
ㅂ **b, p**	ㅅ **s**	ㅇ **ng**	ㅈ **j**	ㅊ **ch**
ㅋ **k**	ㅌ **t**	ㅍ **p**	ㅎ **h**	

DOUBLE CONSONANTS

The tensed (double) consonants are a bit more challenging. The key is to work on using your vocal muscles very strongly, but without expelling air.

English	Korean	Approximate sound in English
kk	ㄲ	as in "s<u>k</u>i, s<u>k</u>y"
tt	ㄸ	as in "s<u>t</u>eak, s<u>t</u>ing"
pp	ㅃ	as in "s<u>p</u>eak, s<u>p</u>y"
ss	ㅆ	as in "<u>s</u>ea, <u>s</u>ir"
jj	ㅉ	as in "bri<u>dg</u>e, mi<u>dg</u>et"

VOWELS

Korean has simple vowels, and dipthongs (combination vowel sounds).

English	Korean	Approximate sound in English
a (*ah*)	ㅏ	as in "f<u>a</u>ther"
eo (*aw*)	ㅓ	as in "f<u>a</u>ll"
o (*oh*)	ㅗ	as in "h<u>o</u>me"
u (*ooh*)	ㅜ	as in "b<u>oo</u>"
eu (*euh*)	ㅡ	as in "tak<u>e</u>n"
i (*ee*)	이	as in "s<u>ee</u>"
ae (*a*)	ㅐ	as in "t<u>a</u>d"
e (*e*)	ㅔ	as in "b<u>e</u>g." This used to differ from **ae** 애, but over time the sounds have become the same, and Koreans say them both exactly the same way most of the time.
oe (*we*)	ㅚ	as in "<u>we</u>lcome"
wi (*wi*)	ㅟ	as in "<u>wee</u>d"
ya (*yah*)	ㅑ	as in "<u>ya</u>rn"
yeo (*yaw*)	ㅕ	as in "<u>yo</u>nder"

English	Korean	Approximate sound in English
yo (*yo*)	ㅛ	as in "<u>yo</u>gurt" (said with a slight pull)
yu (*yu*)	ㅠ	as in "<u>yu</u>le" (said with a slight pull)
yae (ya)	ㅒ	as in "<u>ya</u>k"
ye (ye)	ㅖ	as in "<u>ye</u>s"
wa (*wah*)	ㅘ	as in "<u>wa</u>tch"
wae (*wa*)	ㅙ	as in "<u>wa</u>x"
wo (*wo*)	ㅝ	as in "<u>wo</u>nderful"
we (*weh*)	ㅞ	as in "<u>we</u>dding." The sound value is almost the same as **oe** (*we*). Even Koreans can't always tell the difference.
ui (*ooe*)	의	This is a combination of two sounds, **u** as in "p<u>u</u>ll" followed by **ee** as in "<u>see</u>."

A Note about Written Korean

The Korean writing system is called Hangeul. It requires that any written syllable must begin with a consonant sign. So even when a syllable begins with a vowel sound, you have to write the syllable starting with the zero consonant 0, which has no sound. Like this:

a (*ah*) 아	**u** (*ooh*) 우	**ae** (*a*) 애
eo (*aw*) 어	**eu** (*euh*) 으	**e** (*e*) 에
o (*oh*) 오	**i** (*ee*) 이	**oe** (*we*) 외

1

Traveling

Use 어떻게 말해요? (*eo-ddeo-gae mal-hae-yo?*) to ask "how do you say this in Korean?"

Would you recommend a good place (to travel)?	(yeohaeng hagi) joeun got jom chucheonhae jusillaeyo? *(yawhang hahgee) choh-eun goat chohm choochuhn-hay jooshil-lay-yo?* (여행하기) 좋은 곳 좀 추천해 주실래요?
Have you ever been to Jeju island?	jejudoe gabosyeosseoyo? *jejoo-doh-ay gah-boh-shuss-suh-yo?* 제주도에 가보셨어요?

What is famous at Jeju island?

jejudoeseo mwoga
  yumyeong-haeyo?
*jejoo-doh-ay-suh mwoh-gah
  yoo-myuhng-hay-yo?*
제주도에서 뭐가
  유명해요?

Did you make a reservation?

yeyak hasyeosseoyo?
yay-yahk hah-shuss-uh-yo?
예약하셨어요?

Yes, I made a reservation.

ye, yeyak haesseoyo.
yay, yay-yahk hess-uh-yo.
예, 예약했어요.

No, I didn't make a reservation.

aniyo, yeyak anhaesseoyo.
*ahneeyoh, yay-yahk
  ahn-hess-uh-yo.*
아니요, 예약 안 했어요.

Do you have a room?

bang isseoyo?
bahng iss-uh-yo?
방 있어요?

How long are you going to stay here?

yeogi-e eolma dongan
  gyesil geoyeyo?
*yawgee-ay ull-mah dohng-ahn
  gyeshil guh-yay-yo?*
여기에 얼마 동안
  계실 거예요?

Three nights and four days.

sambak sailiyo.
sahm-bahk sah-eel-eeyo.
삼박 사일이요.

When referring to travel, Koreans will say "a three day, four night trip" or "a one-night, two day trip" rather than just saying the number of days as English people do. So, just put the number of nights in front of 박 (*bahk*) as above and the number of days in front of 일 (*eel*).

A smoking / non-smoking room please.

heubyeonsil / biheubyeonsillo juseyo.
heup-yuhn-shill / bee-heup-yuhn-shil-lo joo-say-yo.
흡연실 / 비흡연실로 주세요.

I'd like to stay another night.

haru deo mukgo sipeoyo.
hah-roo duh mook-goh ship-uh-yo.
하루 더 묵고 싶어요.

Is breakfast included?

achim siksa poham dwae isseoyo?
ah-cheem sheeksah poh-hahm dway iss-uh-yo?
아침식사 포함돼 있어요?

Where can I rent a car / bike?

eodieseo cha / jajeongeoreul billil su (or: renteuhal su) isseoyo?
uh-dee-ay-suh chah / jahjuhn-guhreul bill-ill soo (or: renteu-hahl soo) iss-uh-yo?
어디에서 차 / 자전거를 빌릴 (렌트할) 수 있어요?

In Korea, renting a bicycle at tourist spots is commonplace.

How can I get to the airport / nearest bus stop?

gonghang / jeil gakkaun beo-seu jeongnyuso-kkaji eo-tteoke gayo?

gohng-hahng / jay-eel ga-kkah-oon buh-seu juhng-nyu soh-kkajee uh-tuh-kkay gahyo?

공항 / 제일 가까운 버스 정류소 까지 어떻게 가요?

Where is the most popular place to see a sunrise / sunset?

ilchul / ilmol bol su itneun jeil yumyeonghan gosi eodieyo?

eel-chool / eel-mohl bohl soo een-nohn jay-eel yoo-myung-hahn goh-shee uh-dee-ay-yo?

일출 / 일몰 볼 수 있는 제일 유명한 곳이 어디에요?

How long will it take by car / bus / subway / on foot?

cha / beoseu / jihacheol / doboro eolmana geollyeoyo?

chah / buh-seu / jeehah-chull / dohboh-roh ull-mahnah gull-lyuh-yo?

차 / 버스 / 지하철 / 도보-로 얼마나 걸려요?

Where is the subway / train station?	jihacheolyeoki / gicha cheolyeoki eodiyeyo? *jee-ha-chull yuh-gee / gee-cha-yuh-gee oh-dee-yeh-yoh?* 지하철역이 / 기차역이 어디예요?
Can you call a taxi for me?	taekshi jom bulleojuseyo. *teck-she chohm bool-luh-joo-say-yoh.* 택시 좀 불러주세요.
Where are you going?	eodi gaseyo? *oh-dee gah-say-yoh?* 어디 가세요?
Turn on the meter, please.	miteoreul kyeojuseyo. *mee-taw-reul kyaw-joo-say-yoh.* 미터를 켜주세요.

Time to report someone? Call the Seoul Tourism Complaint Center at 02-735-0101 or a hotline at 120 (press 9 for English).

Could you give me a wakeup call tomorrow morning?	naeil achim moningkol jom hae jusillaeyo? *nay-eel ah-cheem mohn-eeng cawl chohm hay jooshill-lay-yoh?* 내일 아침 모닝콜 좀 해 주실래요?
I'd like to check out.	chekeuaut halgeyo. *check-eu-ah-oot hahlgay-yo.* 체크아웃 할게요.

This is a wonderful view.

yeogi gyeongchi johneyo.
yohgee gyuhng-chee chohnneyo.
여기 경치 좋네요.

This is a nice spot to take a picture.

yeogi sajinjjikgi jonneyo.
yohgee sahjin-jjik-gee chohnneyo.
여기 사진찍기 좋네요.

Would you take a picture of me / us?

(jeo / jeohuideul) sajin jom jji-geojusillaeyo?
(jaw / jaw-hee-deul) sahjin chohm jjee-guh-jooshill-lay-oh?
(저 / 저희들) 사진 좀 찍어주실래요?

Do you want me to take a picture of you?

sajin jjigeodeurilkkayo?
sahjin jjee-guh-deu-rill-kkahyo?
사진 찍어드릴까요?

You can use this same Korean sentence no matter whether you mean "you" as singular (one person) or as plural (a bunch of people). That's because subjects are usually not expressed in Korean sentences.

Do you like it [the picture I've taken]**?**

mame deuseyo?
mah-may deu-say-yo?
맘에 드세요?

Could you take it one more time?

hanbeon deo jjigeo jusillaeyo?
hahnbuhn daw jjee-guh jooshill-lay-oh?
한번 더 찍어 주실래요?

Please count, "one, two, three!"

"hana, dul, set!" hago
    seeo-juseyo.
*"hahnah, dool, set!" hahgoh
    say joo-say-yoh.*
"하나, 둘, 셋~!"하고 세
    주세요.

I'm gonna count to three. One, two, *three*!

setkkaji selgeyo. "hana, dul,
    set!"
*set-kkahjee selgay-yo.
    "hahnah, dool, set!"*
셋까지 셀게요. "하나, 둘,
    셋~!"

You guys look good together. [to a couple]

cham jal eoullisineyo.
*chahm jahl uh-ool-ee-shee-
    nay-yoh.*
참 잘 어울리시네요.

The Korean version of this expression is literally "you match each other well."

Do you have an English-language pamphlet?

yeongeo paempeullit
    isseoyo?
*young-uh pam-peul-lish
    iss-uh-yoh?*
영어 팸플릿 있어요?

Do you have any maps?

jido isseoyo?
jee-do iss-uh-yo?
지도 있어요?

How do I get there?

geogie eoddeohge gayo?
*gaw-gee-ay uh-ttuh-kay
    gah-yoh?*
거기에 어떻게 가요?

2

Getting to Know You

Hello! Hi!	**annyeong (haseyo)!**
	ahn-nyawng (hah-say-yo)!
	안녕 (하세요)!

A simple 안녕 (**annyeong**) is best between close friends or to children, but add the 하세요 (**haseyo**) to coworkers, people you don't know well or strangers.

Allow us to introduce ourselves.	**uri sogae halgeyo.**
	ooree sogay hahl-gay-yo.
	우리 소개할게요.

Would you introduce your friends?	**chingudeul sogae jom hae jushillaeyo?**
	chin-goo-deul sogay chohm hay joo-shill-lay-yo?
	친구들 소개 좀 해 주실래요?

I'm... [name]	**jeoneun...**
	jaw-neun...
	저는…

Where do you live?	**eodi salayo?** *uh-dee sah-lah-yo?* 어디 살아요?
I live in ...	**...eseo salayo.** *...ay-saw sah-lah-yo.* …에서 살아요.
I live in Seoul.	**seouleseo salayo.** *saw-ool-ay-saw sah-lah-yo.* 서울에서 살아요.

The name of Korea's capital city isn't really pronounced like "soul," but rather like "saw-ool" said fairly quickly. Koreans may be confused if you tell them you want to go to "soul."

Where do you come from?	**eodi chulsin iyeyo?** *uh-dee choolsheen ee-ay-yo?* 어디 출신이예요?
I'm from America / the U.K. / Australia / New Zealand.	**jeoneun miguk / yeongguk / hoju / nyujillaendeu eseo wasseoyo.** *jaw-neun meegook / young-gook / hoh-joo / nyu-jeel-land-eu ay-saw wass-uh-yo.* 저는 미국 / 영국 / 호주 / 뉴질랜드에서 왔어요.
How old are you?	**myeot sarieyo? / yeonsega eo-tteoke doeseyo?** *myawt sahlee ay-yo? / yawnsay gah uh-tuh-kkay dwess-ayyo?* 몇 살이에요? / 연세가 어떻게 되세요?

The first option is the more casual way to say it; the second option is the more polite way.

Are you an only child?	**dokja seyo? / oedongttal iseyo?**
	dohk-jah say-yo? / way-dong-ttal eesay-yo?
	독자 세요? (Male) / 외동딸 이세요? (Female)
Are you the oldest?	**(jibeseo) cheotjjae yeyo?**
	(jeeb-ay-suh) chut-jjay yay-yo?
	(집에서) 첫 째예요?
Are you a student?	**haksaeng iseyo?**
	hahksang ee-say-yo?
	학생 이세요?
Where are you studying? (i.e. at what institution)	**eoneu hakgyo daniseyo?**
	aw-neu hahkgyoh dah-nee-say-yo?
	어느 학교 다니세요?
What do (did) you study at the university?	**jeongongi mwoyeyo (mwoyeosseoyo)?**
	juhn-gohng-ee mwo-yay-yo (mwoy-uss-uh-yo)?
	전공이 뭐예요 (뭐였어요)?

I studied economics / law / politics / English / Spanish.

gyeonjae-hak / beop-hak / jeongchi-hak / yeongeo / seupeineo-reul jeongong haesseoyo.

gyawngjay-hahk / buhp-hahk / juhngchee-hahk / young-uh / seupay-ee-nuh-reul juhngohng hess-uh-yo.

경제학 / 법학 / 정치학 / 영어 / 스페인어-를 전공했어요.

What's your job?

jigeobi mwoyeyo?

jee-guh-bi mwo-yeyo?

직업이 뭐예요?

Will you be my Korean teacher?

je hangugeo seonsaengnimi doe jushillaeyo?

jay hahn-goog-uh suhn-sayng-neem-ee dwe joo-shill-lay-yo?

제 한국어 선생님이 돼 주실래요?

I'll teach you English.

jega yeongeo gareuchyeo deurilgeyo.

jay-ga young-uh gahreu-chuh deu-rill-gay-yo.

제가 영어 가르쳐 드릴게요.

**Have I seen you
before?**

uri eodiseo bon jeok ijji
   anayo?
*ooree uh-dee-saw bohn juck
   ee-jjee ah-nah-yo?*
우리 어디서 본 적 있지
   않아요?

**You come here often,
don't you?**

yeogie jaju ojyo, geuchyo?
*yoh-gee-ay jahjoo oh-joh,
   keu-choh?*
여기에 자주 오죠, 그죠?

**I've been watching
you.**

dangsineul gyesok
   barabogo isseosseoyo.
*dahngshin-eul gyay-sohk bah-
   rahboh-goh eessuss-uh-yo.*
당신을 계속 바라보고
   있었어요.

You're really pretty.	jeongmal yeppeu-sineyo. *jawng-mahl yeppeu-sheenay-yo.* 정말 예쁘시네요.
You're handsome.	jeongmal jal saenggi-syeonneyo. *jawng-mahl jahl saynggee-shun-nay-yo.* 정말 잘 생기셨네요.
You're fascinating.	maeryeokjeog-iseyo. *may-ryuhk-juhk-ee-say-yo.* 매력적이세요.
You're sexy.	neo saekshihae. *naw seck-she-hay.* 너 섹시해.
You have a great-looking body.	neon mommaega yebbeo. *nawn mohm-may-gah yeh-baw.* 넌 몸매가 예뻐.
I want to know more about you.	dangsineul jom deo algo sip-eoyo. *dahngshin-eul chohm daw ahlgoh ship-uh-yo.* 당신을 좀 더 알고 싶어요.
You don't talk very much.	mal suga jeogeu-sineyo. *mahl soogah juh-geuh-shee-nay-yo.* 말 수가 적으시네요.

Don't be shy.

bukkeureowo haji malayo.
*boo-kkeuh-rer-wah hahjee
mahlah-yo.*
부끄러워하지 말아요.

**Ask me some
questions.**

jeohante muleobol geo i-
seumumyeon mureo
boseyo.
*jaw-hahn-tay moo-luh-bohl
guh iss-uh-myuhn moo-
luh bohsay-yo.*
저한테 물어볼 거 있으면
물어보세요.

**Ask me anything
you want.**

muleo bogo sipeun geo
amugeona mureo
boseyo.
*moo-luh boh-goh ship-eun
guh ahmooguhna moo-luh
boh-say-yo.*
물어 보고 싶은 거
아무거나 물어보세요.

**Except what color
underwear I'm
wearing.**

je sogot saek-kkalman
ppae-guyo.
*jay sohk-oat seck-kkahl-mahn
ppay-gooyo.*
제 속옷 색깔만 빼구요.

I like your personality.

seonggyeogi cham joeu-
sineyo.
*suhng-gyuhg-ee chahm choh-
euh-shee-nay-yo.*
성격이 참 좋으시네요.

You're my type.

___ ssi-neun je taibieyo. / neoneun nae taibiya.

___ sshee-neun jay tah-eebee-ay-yo. / naw-neun nae tah-eebee-yah.

___ 씨는 제 타입이에요. / 너는 내 타입이야.

The first option is the more polite way to say it; the second option is the more casual way.

Start the sentence with the person's name, followed by the suffix **-ssi**. Korean people tend not to call someone "you" or say "your" unless the person is close enough. Instead, they use his / her name with **-ssi**. For example, the idea of "your car" would instead be said as "[name]-**ssi** car," and "your friends" as "[name]-**ssi** friends."

What kind of people do you like?

eotteon sarameul joa haseyo?

aw-ttuhn sahrahm-eul choh-ah hah-say-yo?

어떤 사람을 좋아하세요?

I like a/an ... type of person.

... taibeul joa haeyo.

... taheeb-eul choh-ah hay-yo.

⋯ 타입을 좋아해요.

quiet

joyonghan

choh-yong-hahn

조용한

loud

sikkeureoun

shee-kkeu-ruh-oon

시끄러운

tender

budeureoun

boo-deu-ruh-oon

부드러운

funny	**jaemi itneun**
	jehm-ee eet-neun
	재미있는
sincere / dedicated	**jinjunghan / heonsin-jeogin**
	jinjoong-hahn / huhn-shin-
	juhgeen
	진중한 / 헌신적인
considerate	**saryeo gipeun**
	sahryaw geepeun
	사려깊은
introverted	**naeseongjeokin**
	nay-suhng-juhk-in
	내성적인
extroverted	**hwaldongjeokin**
	hwahl-dong-juhk-in
	활동적인
stylish	**seutaillisihan**
	seu-tah-eel-lee-shee-hahn
	스타일리시한
slim	**nalssinhan**
	nalssheen-hahn
	날씬한
big	**deongchiga keun**
	duhngchee-gah keun
	덩치가 큰
big eyes	**nuni keun**
	noonee keun
	눈이 큰

small	jageun *jahgeun* 작은
small butt	eongdeongiga jageun *uhng-duhng-ee-gah jahgeun* 엉덩이가 작은
small breasts	gaseumi jageun *gahseu-mee jahgeun* 가슴이 작은
small mouth	ibi jageun *eebee jahgeun* 입이 작은
I like your hairstyle.	heeo seutail yeppe usineyo. *hair seu-tah-eel yepp eu-shee-nay-yo.* 헤어스타일 예쁘시네요.
Do you follow the latest fads?	yuhaeng-e mingam haseyo? *yuhayng-ee meengahm hah-say-yo?* 유행에 민감하세요?
What's popular now?	yojeum yuhaeng-i mwoyeyo? *yojeum yuhayng-ee mwo-yay-yo?* 요즘 유행이 뭐예요?

You have good taste in clothes.

ot ipneun gamgagi joeusineyo.

ohsh eem-neun gahmgahg-ee choh-euh-shee-nay-yo.

옷 입는 감각이 좋으시네요.

I'm not very stylish.

jeoneun byeollo seutaillisi haji anayo.

jaw-neun byawl-loh seu-tah-eel-leeshee hahjee ahnahyo.

저는 별로 스타일리시 하지 않아요.

Shall we go shopping together someday?

eonje syoping gachi galkkayo?

awn-jay shoh-peeng gahchee gahl-kkayo?

언제 쇼핑 같이 갈까요?

I don't like to shop alone.

jeoneun honja syoping haneun geol an joa haeyo.

jaw-neun hohn-jah shoh-peeng hahneun gull ahn choh-ah hay-yo.

저는 혼자 쇼핑하는 걸 안 좋아해요.

Do you have a steady boyfriend / girlfriend?

orae sagwin namchin / yeochin isseoyo?

awray sahgwin nahm-cheen / yaw-cheen iss-uh-yo?

오래 사귄 남친 / 여친 있어요?

You must be very popular.	inkki maneusil geot gatayo. *in-kki mah-neu-shill guht gahtah-yo.* 인기 많으실 것 같아요.
You must have a girlfriend.	yeochin isseul geot gatayo. *yaw-cheen ee-sseul guht gahtah-yo.* 여친 있을 것 같아요.
You must have a boyfriend.	namchin isseul geot gatayo. *nahm-cheen ee-sseul guht gahtah-yo.* 남친 있을 것 같아요.
Yes, I had one, but we've just broken up.	(yeochin / namchin) isseotneunde, eolma jeon-e kkaejyeosseoyo. *(yaw-cheen / nahm-cheen) ee-ssuhn-neun-day, ull-mah juhn-ay kkay-juss-uh-yo.* (여친 / 남친) 있었는데, 얼마 전에 깨졌어요.

Say the first—**yeochin**—if you had a girlfriend; say **namchin** if you had a boyfriend.

I've never dated a Korean boy / girl before.	hanguk namja / yeoja hago deiteuhae bon jeok eopseoyo. *hahn-gook nahm-jah / yaw-jah hahgo day-ee-teuh-hay bohn juhk up-suh-yo.* 한국 남자 / 여자하고 데이트해 본 적 없어요.

Will you go out with me?	**jeohago gachi nagasillaeyo?** *jaw-hah-goh gahchee nahga-shill-lay-yo?* 저하고 같이 나가실래요?
Do you believe in destiny?	**unmyeongeul mideuseyo?** *oon-muhng-eul meedeuh-say-yo?* 운명을 믿으세요?
Let's do this again.	**igeo daeume tto haeyo.** *ee-guh dah-eum-ay tto hay-yo.* 이거 다음에 또 해요.
Let's get together later.	**daeume han beon tto moijyo.** *dah-eum-ay hahn buhn tto moh-ee-jyo.* 다음에 한 번 또 모이죠.

Say this when the "us" is three or more people.

Let's see each other again.	**daeume tto bwayo.** *dah-oom-ay tto bwahyo.* 다음에 또 봐요.

Say this when the "us" is two or more people.

Let's meet on Tuesday at your favorite café.	___ ssi-ga jeil joa haneun ka-peeseo daeum ju hwayoilnal mannalkkayo? *___ sshee-gah jay-eel choh-ah hahneun kkah-pay-ay-suh dah-eum joo hwa-yo-eel mahn-nahl-kka-yo?* ___ 씨가 제일 좋아하는 카페에서 다음 주 화요일에 만날까요?

Start the sentence with the person's name, followed by the suffix **-ssi**.

Monday	**wolyoil** *wool-yoh-ill* 월요일
Tuesday	**hwayoil** *hwah-yoh-ill* 화요일
Wednesday	**suyoil** *soo-yoh-ill* 수요일
Thursday	**mokyoil** *mohk-yoh-ill* 목요일
Friday	**geumyoil** *geum-yoh-ill* 금요일

Saturday

toyoil
toh-yoh-ill
토요일

Sunday

ilyoil
ill-yoh-ill
일요일

I'm glad we met.

mannaseo bangawoyo.
mahn-nahsuh bahn-gah-
wah-yo.
만나서 반가워요.

It'd be great to see you again.

dasi mannasseumyeon jo-
ketneyo.
dahshee mahn-nahss-eu-
myuhn choh-ken-nay-yo.
다시 만났으면 좋겠네요.

Fun and Games

Are you busy right now?	jigeum bappayo? *chig-eum bah-ppah-yoh?* 지금 바빠요?
What shall we do now?	uri ije mwo halkkayo? *ooree eejay mwo hahl-kkah- yoh?* 우리 이제 뭐 할까요?
I want to go to...	...e gago sipeoyo. *...ay gah-goh ship-uh-yo.* ...에 가고 싶어요.
I like...	...(eul / reul) joa haeyo. *...(eul / reul) joh-ah hay-yo.* ...(을 / 를) 좋아해요.
What do you want to do?	mwo hago sipeoyo? *mwo hah-goh ship-uh-yo?* 뭐 하고 싶어요?

What do your friends want to do?	___ ssi chingu-deuleun mwo hago sipdaeyo? *___ sshee chin-goo-deul-eun mwo hah-goh ship-day-yo?* ___ 씨 친구들은 뭐 하고 싶대요?

Start the sentence with the person's name, followed by the suffix **-ssi**. Korean people tend not to call someone "you" or say "your" unless the person is close enough. Instead, they use his / her name with **-ssi**. For example, the idea of "your car" would instead be said as "[name]-**ssi** car," and "your friends" as "[name]-**ssi** friends."

Let's (all) go out together.	**uri da gachi nagayo.** *ooree dah gahchee nahgahyo.* 우리 다 같이 나가요.
Let's leave together.	**uri gachi tteonayo.** *ooree gahchee ttuh-nahyo.* 우리 같이 떠나요.
It'll be a lot of fun.	**jinjja jaemi isseul geoyeyo.** *jeen-jjah jehm-ee isseul guh-yay-yo.* 진짜 재미있을 거예요.
Let's go to the beach.	**haebyeon-euro gayo.** *hay-byuhn-eur-oh gahyo.* 해변으로 가요.
Let's go to a baseball / soccer game.	**yagu / chukgu boreo gayo.** *yahgoo / chookgoo boh-raw gahyo.* 야구 / 축구 보러 가요.

What's the local team here?	**yeogi homtim-i museun tim-ieyo?** *yawgee hohm-teem-ee moo-seun teem-ee-ay-yo?* 여기 홈 팀이 무슨 팀이에요?
Let's go cheer our team!	**uri tim eungwon halkkayo?** *ooree teem eungwon hahlkkah-yoh?* 우리 팀 응원할까요?
I've always wanted to go to Jamsil Ball Park / Munhak Ball Park.	**jamsil gujang / munhak gujang e hangsang ga bogo sipeosseoyo.** *Jahmshill goojahng / moonhahk goojahng ay hahnsahng gah boh-goh ship-uss-uh-yo.* 잠실 구장 / 문학 구장에 항상 가 보고 싶었어요.

Jamsil **gujang** (ball park) is in Seoul, and Munhak **gujang** is in Incheon. Munhak was built more recently than Jamsil, so Munhak has a more modern facility. On the other hand, Jamsil is located in one of the most popular districts in Seoul.

Go! Go for it!	**faiting!** *fah-eeteeng!* 파이팅!

As you can probably guess, this phrase came from the English word "fighting!"

Who is that (player)?	**jeo seonsu nugu-yeyo?** *jaw suhnsoo noogoo-yay-yo?* 저 선수 누구예요?

Let's watch a movie.	**yeonghwa boreo gayo.** *young-hwah boh-ruh gahyo.* 영화 보러 가요.
Did you see...?	**... bwasseoyo?** *... bwah-ssuh-yo?* ⋯ 봤어요?
I saw (it).	**bwasseoyo.** *bwah-ssuh-yo.* 봤어요.
I didn't see (it).	**an bwasseoyo.** *ahn bwah-ssuh-yo.* 안 봤어요.
I couldn't see (it).	**mot bwasseoyo.** *moht bwah-ssuh-yo.* 못 봤어요.
I don't want to see (it).	**(geugeo) bogi silheoyo.** *(geuguh) bohgee shill-uh-yo.* (그거) 보기 싫어요.
Do you want to see...?	**... bosil-laeyo?** *... boh-shill-lay-yo?* ⋯ 보실래요?
Shall we go and watch it?	**geugeo boreo galkkayo?** *(geuguh) boh-ruh gahl-kkahyo?* 그거 보러 갈까요?

What time does the next [movie, game, etc.] start?	daeum [yeonghwa, geim, etc.] eonje sijak haeyo? *dah-eum [young-hwah gay-eem, etc.] uhn-jay shee-jahk hay-yo?* 다음 〔영화, 게임 etc.〕 언제 시작해요?
We have plenty of time.	uri sigan manayo. *ooree sheegahn mah-nahyo.* 우리 시간 많아요.
Shall we get a video / DVD (instead)?	(daesine) bidio / dibidi bol kkayo? *(day-sheen-ay) beedee-o / dee-beedee bohl-kkahyo?* (대신에) 비디오 / 디비디 볼까요?

In Korea, renting a movie is a popular pastime and you can find a lot of video / DVD rental stores.

Shall we go to a DVD *bang*?	uri dibidibange kalkkayo? *ooree dee-bee-dee bahng-ay kahl-kkah-yo?* 우리 디비디방에 갈까요?
Let's watch a movie at a DVD *bang*!	uri dibidibangeseo yeonghwareul bolkkayo? *ooree dee-bee-dee bahng-ay-saw young-hwah-reul bohl-kkah-yo?* 우리 디비디방에서 영화를 볼까요?

A DVD *bang* (room) is a private room to watch the movie of your choice. It's a great place for a couple to get some alone time, away from their parents.

Do you know a good place (near here)?

(i geuncheo e) gwaen-
  chaneun de alayo?
*(ee geun-chaw-ay) gwen-
  chahn-eun day ahlahyo?*
(이 근처에) 괜찮은 데
  알아요?

I know (a good place).

(joeun de) alayo.
(choh-eun day) ahlahyo.
(좋은 데) 알아요.

Do you like karaoke?

noraebangeul jo-a-haeyo?
*nohray-bahng-eul choh-a-
  hay-yo?*
노래방을 좋아해요?

Karaoke is alive and well in Korea; Korean people generally love
to sing. They often go to karaoke after drinks with friends.

Let's go to a karaoke room.

noraebange gaseo
  noraehaeyo.
*nohray-bahng-ay gah-saw
  nohray-hay-yo.*
노래방에 가서 노래해요.

What shall we sing first?

museun norae halkkayo?
*mooseun nohray hahl-kkah-
  yo?*
무슨 노래 할까요?

You choose the first song (You go first).	cheotbeonjjae gok goreuseyo (meonjeo haseyo). *chuht-buhn-jjay gohk goh-reu-say-yo (muhn-juh hah-say-yo).* 첫번째 곡 고르세요 (먼저 하세요).
Are there any English songs?	pap song (yeong eo norae) isseoyo? *pahp sohng (young-uh noh-ray) iss-uh-yo?* 팝송 (영어 노래) 있어요?

Either option is fine: **pap song** means the English phrase "pop song," and **yeong eo norae** means "English song." There are usually plenty of them in the book, sometimes in a special section, and sometimes mixed in with the Korean songs.

I don't know how to work the machine.	i gigyereul eotteoke jakdong haneun ji mollayo. *ee gee-gyay-reul uh-tuh-kkay jahk-dohng hahneun jee mohl-lahyo.* 이 기계를 어떻게 작동하는지 몰라요.

That person's / John's singing is funny / interesting.

jeo saram-i / Jon-i bureuneun norae utgineyo / jaeminneyo.
jaw sahrahm-ee / jahn-ee boo-reu-neun nohray oot-gee-nay-yo / jehm-een-nay-yo.
저 사람 / 존 이 부르는 노래 웃기네요 / 재미있네요.

Shall we sing something together?

uri da gachi han gok bureul-kkayo?
ooree dah gahchee hahn gohk boo-reul-kkah-yo?
우리 다 같이 한 곡 부를까요?

Your singing is really good.

norae cham jal hasineyo.
noh-ray chahm jahl hah-shee-nay-yo.
노래 참 잘하시네요.

Shall we go shopping?

syoping galkkayo?
shoh-peeng gahl-kkah-yo?
쇼핑 갈까요?

I want to go shopping for clothes.

ot sareo gago sipeoyo.
oht sahruh gah-goh ship-uh-yo.
옷 사러 가고 싶어요.

Let's go to (shopping at) Migliore / Myeongdong.	Mileore / Myeong-dong e (syo-ping hareo) gago sipeoyo.

Meel-lee-oh-reh / Myuhng-dohng ay (shoh-peeng hah-ruh) gah-goh ship-uh-yo.

밀리오레 / 명동에 (쇼핑하러) 가고 싶어요.

Migliore is a department store, and you can find good prices on clothing there. Myeongdong is in the heart of downtown Seoul, and is a major shopping district—a bit like 5th Avenue in New York.

Let's go to Everland.	Everlande galkkayo?

Everland-ay gahl-kkah-yo?

에버랜드에 갈까요?

Everland, about an hour from Seoul, is a popular amusement park, Korea's largest; many find it similar to the Disney resort experience. For something in Seoul, take the subway to Lotte World (롯데 월드) and its mostly indoor amusement park.

I hear it's a good spot for a date.	geogiga deiteu hagi-e anseong-machum iradeon-deyo. *gaw-gee-gah deh-ee-teu hahgee-ay ahnsuhng-mahchoom eerah-duhn-day-yo.* 거기가 데이트하기에 안성맞춤이라던데요.
Let's go to the park again.	geu gongwon-e tto gayo. *geu gohngwon-eh ttoh gahyo.* 그 공원에 또 가요.
I love to hold your hand as we walk through the park.	___ ssi son japgo gongwon sanchaek hago sipeoyo. *___ sshee sohn jahpgoh gohng won sahncheck hah-goh ship-uh-yo.* ___ 씨 손 잡고 공원 산책하고 싶어요.

Start the sentence with the person's name, followed by the suffix **-ssi**. Remember, Korean people tend not to call someone "you" or say "your" unless the person is close enough.

I came here by car.	yeogie charo wasseoyo. *yaw-gee-ay chah-roh wassuh-yo.* 여기에 차로 왔어요.
Would you like to go for a drive?	deurai-beureul gallaeyo? *deu-rah-ee-beu-reul gahl-lay-yo?* 드라이브를 갈래요?

I have room for two more of your friends.	___ ssi chingudeul dumyeong deo tal su isseoyo.
	___ sshee chin-goo-deul doo myuhng duh tahl soo iss-uh-yo.
	___ 씨 친구들 두명 더 탈 수 있어요.

Start the sentence with the person's name, followed by the suffix **-ssi**. Remember, Korean people tend not to call someone "you" or say "your" unless the person is close enough. Instead, they use his / her name with **-ssi**.

4

Eating and Drinking

Would you like something to drink?

mwo masil geot jom deuril-kkayo?

mwo mahshill guht chohm deu-rill-kkahyo?

뭐 마실 것 좀 드릴까요?

Let's get some food.

mwo jom meokjyo.

mwo chohm mawk-jyo.

뭐 좀 먹죠.

The menu please.

menyu juseyo.

menyu joosay-yo.

메뉴 주세요.

What do you want (to eat)?

mwo deusillaeyo?

mwo deu-shill-lay-yo?

뭐 드실래요?

I'm a vegetarian.

jeoneun chaesik juuija yeyo.

jaw-neun chay-shik joo-ooey-jah yay-yoh.

저는 채식주의자예요.

I can't eat …	**… mot meokeoyo.**
	… moht mawg-aw-yoh.
	… 못먹어요.
I'm allergic to … .	**jeo-neun … al-le-reu-gi-ga issoyo.**
	jaw-neun … ahl-lay-reu-gee-gah iss-uh-yo.
	저는 … 알레르기가 있어요.
Without …	**bbaego …**
	bay-goh …
	… 빼고

Add in the thing you're allergic to or can't eat: milk −우유 (*oo-yoo*), eggs −계란 (*gye-ran*), peanuts −땅콩 (*ddang-kong*), nuts −넛 (*neot*, sounds like 'nut,' refers to nuts in general), wheat −밀 (*mil*), and meat −고기 (*go-gi*).

What do you recommend?	**yeo-gi mwo-ga je-il masiss-eo-yo?**
	yaw-gee mwoh-gah jay-ill mahsh-iss-uh-yoh?
	여기 뭐가 제일 맛있어요?
Is it spicy?	**mae-wo-yo?**
	mae-wah-yo?
	매워요?
Please make it less spicy.	**maeb-ji an-ge hae ju-se-yo).**
	mehb-jee ahn-gay hae joo-say-yo).
	맵지 않게 해 주세요.

I'll order (for us).	**jega jumun halkkeyo.** *jaygah joomoon hahl-kkay-yo.* 제가 주문할게요.
I'll buy it.	**jega nehlkeyo.** *jaygah nehl-kkay-yo.* 제가 낼게요.
Try this!	**igeo meogeo / deusyeo boseyo.** *ee-guh muh-guh / deu-shaw boh-say-yo.* 이거 먹어 / 드셔 보세요.

Say the first option when you prefer to be more casual, and the second option when you want to be more polite.

I've never tried this.	**igeo han beondo an meogeo bwasseoyo.** *ee-guh hahn buhn-doh ahn maw-guh bwahss-uh-yo.* 이거 한 번도 안 먹어 봤어요.
What's your favorite Korean food?	**hanguk eumsik jungeseo jeil joahaneun ge mwoyeyo?** *hahngook eumsheek joong- ay-saw jay-eel jo-ah- hahneun guh mwo-yay- yo?* 한국 음식 중에서 제일 좋아하는 게 뭐예요?

It's obviously impossible to cover the vast scope of Korean cuisine in this book, so your best bet is to just get out there and try some of it for yourself! Some common favorites include: *bibimbap* 비빔밥 (rice mixed with vegetables, red pepper sauce, and often beef / eggs), *galbi* 갈비 (barbecued ribs), *kimbap* 김밥 (rice with vegetables and one of several types of meat wrapped in seaweed), *samgyeopsal* 삼겹살 (barbecued pork belly), and *jja-jangmyeon* 짜장면 (noodles with black bean sauce). Some common anything-but-favorites include *hongeo* 홍어 (fermented skate that smells like a chemical disaster and has a taste to match), *beondegi* 번데기 (cooked silkworm larvae), and *boshintang* 보신탕 (dog soup—this has gone underground to a very large extent, but you can still find a 보신탕 restaurant without too much difficulty if you look around a few back alleys).

I like …	**jega …eul / reul choahaeyo.** *jay-gah …eul / reul choh-ah-hay-yo.* 제가 ⋯을 / 를 좋아해요.

Use **eul** (을) after words ending in consonants, and **reul** (를) after words ending in vowels.

I like samgyeopsal.	**jega samgyeopsaleul choahaeyo.** *jay-gah sahm-gyuhp-sahl-eul choh-ah-hay-yo.* 제가 삼겹살을 좋아해요.
I like kimchi.	**jega gimchireul choahaeyo.** *jay-gah kim-chee-reul choh-ah-hay-yo.* 제가 김치를 좋아해요.
What is this called?	**i-geo i-reum-i mwo-ye-yo?** *ee-gaw ee-reum-ee mwoh-yeh-yoh?* 이거 이름이 뭐예요?

Can you eat...?

… meogeul su isseoyo?
… muh-geul soo ee-ssuh-yo?
… 먹을 수 있어요?

Yes, I can.

ye, meogeul su isseoyo.
yay, muh-geul soo ee-ssuh-yo.
예, 먹을 수 있어요.

No, I can't.

aniyo, motmeogeoyo.
ahneeyo, moht-maw-guh-yo.
아니요, 못 먹어요.

(That) looks delicious.

masi-sseul geot gatneyo.
*mahsh-ees-eul guht gahd-
    neyo.*
맛있을 것 같네요.

Give me a bit more.

jogeum deo juseyo.
chohgeum duh joo-say-yo.
조금 더 주세요.

Gimme more.

jom deo juseyo.
chohm duh joo-say-yo.
좀 더 주세요.

Enough.

chungbunhaeyo.
choong-boon-hay-yo.
충분해요.

Enough?

chungbunhaeyo?
choong-boon-hay-yo?
충분해요?

Not enough?

bujok haeyo?
boojohk hay-yo?
부족해요?

(Sorry,) I can't eat that.   (joesong hajiman) geugeoneun motmeogeul geot
gatayo.
*(chay-sohng hah-jee-mahn)
geu-gaw-neun mon-maw-
geul guht gahtahyo.*
(죄송하지만,) 그거는 못
먹을 것 같아요.

Literally translated, the next statement means "I will eat this well."
This is a common polite thing to say before you eat food,
especially when you're invited to someone's home.

jal meokkesseupnida.
jahl muhkkesseum-ni-da.
잘 먹겠습니다.

What do you think   ige eottaeyo?
(about this)?   *ee-gay uh-ttay-yo?*
이게 어때요?

Does this taste good?   ige masisseoyo?
ee-gay masheess-uh-yo?
이게 맛있어요?

It tastes good.   masitneyo.
masheen-neyo.
맛있네요.

It's an unusual taste.   teugihan masineyo.
teu-geehahn mahshee-nay-yo.
특이한 맛이네요.

It's O.K. / so-so.

gwaenchanayo / goman goman haneyo.
gwen-chah-nahyo / gohmahn gohmahn hah-nay-yo.
괜찮아요 / 고만고만 하네요.

It's not good.

byeolloyeyo.
byull-loh-yay-yo.
별로예요.

It doesn't taste good.

masi eopseoyo.
mashee up-suh-yo.
맛이 없어요.

It's awful.

jinjja madeopseoyo.
chinn-jjah maht up-suh-yo.
진짜 맛없어요.

I'm full.

bae bul-leo-yo.
bay bool-luh-yo.
배 불러요.

You can say this after you've eaten, especially when you're eating in someone's home. It literally means "I ate this well."

jal meogeotsseumnida.
jahl maw-guss-sseum-nee-da.
잘 먹었습니다.

If you're thinking it looks a lot like 잘 먹겠습니다, the expression you just learned, you're right; they're exactly the same except that the first is in the future tense since you'll be eating well, and the second is in the past tense since you already ate well.

Do you smoke?

dambae piuseyo?
dahmbay pee-oo-say-yo?
담배 피우세요?

This is a non-smoking section.

yeogineun geumyeon guyeogieyo.
yawgee-neun geum-yawn goo-yawg-ee-ay-yo.
여기는 금연구역이에요.

Could you bring me an ashtray?

jaetteoli jom gatta jusigesseoyo?
jay-tteulee chohm gahttah jooshee-gess-uh-yo?
재떨이 좀 갖다 주시겠어요?

Do you drink (alcohol)?

sul mashiseyo?
sool mah-shee-say-yo?
술 마시세요?

How much can you drink?

juryang-i eotteoke doeseyo?
joo-ryang-ee uh-ttuh-kay dweh-say-yo?
주량이 어떻게 되세요?

(I can drink) half a bottle of soju.

soju ban byeongiyo.
sohjoo bahn byuhng-eeyo.
소주 반 병이요.

Comparable to vodka but not as potent, **soju** is the most popular traditional Korean liquor. It's between 15-20% ABV, with some varieties reaching 40%! In Korea it's usually made from sweet potatoes. **Soju** is usually served in shot glasses and drunk while eating.

Remember that it's a traditional custom in Korea to never fill your own glass. Instead, someone else at the table should fill it for you.

**Do you drink beer /
soju / wine /
strong liquor?**

maekju / soju / wain /
dokan sul mashiseyo?
*mehkjoo / sohwjoo /
wah-een / dohkhahn sool
mah-shee-say-yo?*
맥주 / 소주 / 와인 / 독한
술 마시세요?

Bottled beer please.

byeong maekju juseyo.
byuhng mehkjoo joo-say-yo.
병맥주 주세요.

Draft beer please.

saeng maekju juseyo.
sayng mehkjoo joo-say-yo.
생맥주 주세요.

Can we buy beer here?

yeogi maekju pallyeoyo?
yawgee mehkjoo pahl-lyuh-yo?
여기 맥주 팔려요?

**The drinks here
taste terrible.**

yeogineun sul masi an
joayo.
*yawgee-neun sool mahshee
ahn choh-ah-yo.*
여기는 술 맛이 안
좋아요.

This is not very strong.

i suleun yakhaneyo.
ee sooleun yahk-hah-nay-yo.
이 술은 약하네요.

Drink up!

won syat!
One shot!
원 샷~!

As you might guess, this expression comes from the English
words "one shot."

Cheers!	**geonbae!**
	guhn-bay!
	건배!

What kind of anju do you want with the drink?	**anjuneun mwollo halkkayo?**
	ahnjoo-neun mwol-loh hahl-kkah-yoh?
	안주는 뭘로 할까요?

In Korea, **anju** is the name for the food / snacks people eat while they drink alcohol. Some **anju** comes free with your drink(s), while more substantial **anju** usually costs money.

Dried anju, please.	**mareun anju juseyo.**
	mahreun ahnjoo joo-say-yo.
	마른 안주 주세요.

Dried **anju** would include foods like dried squid, peanuts, etc.

Fruit anju, please.	**gwail anju juseyo.**
	gwah-eel ahnjoo joo-say-yo.
	과일 안주 주세요.

As a rule of thumb, any **anju** that isn't a snacky sort of finger food will probably cost you something.

Fried chicken, please.	**huraideu chikin juseyo.**
	hoo-rah-ee-deu chicken joo-say-yo.
	후라이드 치킨 주세요.

I'm getting drunk.	**chwihaneyo.**
	chwee-hah-nay-yo.
	취하네요.

I'm drunk.	**chwi-haesseoyo.**
	chwee-hess-uh-yo.
	취했어요.

**You are a good
drinker** (You can
really hold your
liquor).

___ ssi sul ssesineyo.
____ sshee sool sseh-shee-
nay-yo._
씨 술 세시네요.

Start the sentence with the person's name, followed by the suffix
-ssi.

**You're not much of a
drinker.**

___ ssi suli yakhasineyo.
____ sshee soolee yahk-hah-
shee-nay-yo._
씨 술이 약하시네요.

Start the sentence with the person's name, followed by the suffix
-ssi.

Don't just eat anju
(Drink alcohol
as well)!

anjuppal jom geuman
seuseyo!
_ahn-jooppahl chohm geu-
mahn say-oo-say-yo!_
안주빨 좀 그만 세우세요!

I'll fill your glass up.

je sul han jan badeuseyo.
_jay sool hahn jahn bah-
deu-say-yo._
제 술 한 잔 받으세요.

In Korea, you should fill the other party's glass whenever it's
empty, as a courtesy. Again, don't fill your own!

Check, please!

gye-san-seo ju-se-yo.
gyay-sahn-suh joo-say-yo.
계산서 주세요.

I'll treat you.

jega naelkkeyo / nega ssol-
kke.

*jay-gah nell-kkay-yo / jay-gah
ssohl-kkay.*

제가 낼게요 / 내가 쏠게

The first option is standard Korean speech; the next is slang.

**Separate checks,
please.**

ta-ro ta-ro hae juseyo.

ta-ro ta-ro hay joo-say-yo.

타로타로 해 주세요.

Let's split the bill.

gachi naelkkayo.

gahchee nell-kkah-yo.

같이 낼까요.

**Do you accept
credit cards?**

sinyongkadeudo dwaeyo?

*shinyohng-kah-deu-doh
dway-yo?*

신용카드도 돼요?

I lost my wallet.

jigabeul ilheobeo-
ryeosseoyo.

*jee-gahb-eul eel-uh-burr-
yussuh-yo.*

지갑을 잃어버렸어요.

**I don't have any
money.**

doni eopseoyo.

dohnee up-suh-yo.

돈이 없어요.

**Can I borrow
20,000 won?**

i(2) manwonman billyeo
jusil-laeyo?

*ee(2) mahnwon-mahn bill-yuh
jooshill-lay-oh?*

이(2) 만원만 빌려
주실래요?

Let's move to another bar (pub, karaoke, etc.)

icha / samchae gajyo.
eecha / samcha ay gah-jyoh.
이차 / 삼차에 가죠~!

In this situation, instead of "another," you say 이차 (**icha**) which means "the second," or 삼차 (**samcha**) which means "the third." If later you want to go to still another pub or karaoke, you can say 사차 (**sacha**) which literally translates as "the fourth place."

Let's drink 'til we die!

sul meokgo jukja!
sool mug-goh jookjah!
술 먹고 죽자~!

This is an often-heard joking phrase that's used to make the atmosphere relaxed and enjoyable when people drink together.

Please call a taxi.

taeksireul jom bulleojuseyo.
*teck-shee-reul chohm
  bool-luh-joo-say-yo.*
택시를 좀 불러주세요.

I've got a hangover.

sukchwiga isseoyo.
sook-chwi-ga iss-uh-yo.
숙취가 있어요.

I have a splitting headache.

meoriga kkaejil geot gatayo.
*muh-reega kkaejill guht
  gahtahyo.*
머리가 깨질 것 같아요.

My stomach hurts.

sok sseuryeoyo.
sohk sseu-ryaw-yo.
속 쓰려요.

I feel nausea.

tohal geot gatayo.
toh-hahl guht gahtahyo.
토할 것 같아요.

I feel like vomiting /
I'm about to vomit.
	obaiteu ssollyeoyo /
	    neomeo-ol geot gatayo.
	awbah-ee-teuh ssohl-lyaw-yo /
	    nuh-muh-ohl guht
	    gahtahyo.
	오바이트 쏠려요 / 넘어올
	    것 같아요.

I (have) vomited.	tohaesseoyo / meogeun geo
	    da hwaginhaesseoyo.
	toh-hess-uh-yo / maw-geun
	    guh dah hwah-geen-hess-
	    uh-yo.
	토했어요. / 먹은 거 다
	    확인했어요.

Tohaesseoyo is the more normal way to say it; **Meogeun geo da hwaginhaesseoyo** is slang which literally means, "I've checked everything I ate."

You drank too much
last night,
didn't you?
	eoje sul mani masyeotjyo,
	    geureotchyo?
	uh-jay sool mani ma-shuht-
	    jyo, geu-ruht-chyo?
	어제 술 많이 마셨죠,
	    그렇죠?

Let's go get some
haejangguk.
	haejangguk meogeureo
	    gajyo.
	hay-jahng-gook maw-geu-ruh
	    gah-jyo.
	해장국 먹으러 가죠.

Koreans usually eat **Haejangguk**, anti-hangover soup, the next morning. It's popularly believed to help you recover.

I blacked out.

pilleum-i kkeungyeosseoyo.
pill-leum-ee kkeun-gyuss-
  uh-yo.
필름이 끊겼어요.

This interesting Korean expression literally means "The film is cut."
The film, in this case, is your memory.

**Did I make any
  mistakes (last
  night)?**

**(eojet bame) jega silsuhan
  ge eopseoyo?**
(uh-jet bahm-ay) jay-gah
  shillsoo-hahn gay up-suh-
  yo?
(어젯밤에) 제가 실수한
  게 없어요?

5

Clubbing

In Korea nightlife is an ever-evolving sort of thing, but traditionally in Seoul it's been focused around two areas—Itaewon and Hongdae.

The former is the expat district, known for shops of cheap knockoff souvenirs and plenty of good food from around the world. Just down the road from Itaewon is an area called Haebangchon, a sort of center for the more creative expat crowd which starts around Noksapyeong Station and continues up the hill. Haebangchon also has plenty of great restaurants. Both Itaewon and Haebangchon have a lot of little bars where you can see expat bands play, and there are occasional trivia or comedy nights as well—keep your eyes on the local English magazines to find out what's happening on any given weekend.

Hongdae is more of a mix of expats and Koreans and has more dance clubs and the like, as well as smaller bars with live music. You can find everything from jazz to swing, old-fashioned rock 'n' roll, punk, techno, and even metal. Again, check out local magazines or ask your friends—you're sure to find something there to suit you.

For those who prefer something a little more elegant (with prices to match) the Apgujeong and Gangnam areas also have plenty of clubs where the beautiful people like to be seen—there's a reason Psy lampooned Gangnam as the home of the upscale and fashionable in his famous song.

Let's go to a nightclub.	naiteuro galggayo? *nah-ee-teu-roh gahl-gah-yo?* 나이트로 갈까요?
Let's go to your favorite club.	___ ssi-ga jeil joahaneun keul-leobe galggayo. *___ sshee-gah jay-eel choh-ah-hahneun keul-luhb-ay gahlggah-yo?* ___ 씨가 제일 좋아하는 클럽에 갈까요?

Start the sentence with the person's name, followed by the suffix **-ssi**.

I've never been to a club.	jeon keulleobe gabon jeogi eopseoyo. *jawn keul-luhb-ay gah-bohn juhgee up-suh-yo.* 전 클럽에 가 본 적이 없어요.
How much is the admission?	ipjangryoga eolmayeyo? *eep-jahng-nyo-gah ull-mah-yay-yo?* 입장료가 얼마예요?
Are you waiting in line?	jul seo isseuseyo? *jool saw eess-eu-say-yo?* 줄 서 있으세요?

You wait here.

yeogieseo gidariseyo.
*yaw-gee-ehsuh geedahree-
    say-yo.*
여기에서 기다리세요.

I'll do it.

jega halkkeyo.
jay-gah hahl-kkay-yo.
제가 할게요.

**Are there many
    hot girls / handsome
    guys in the club?**

geu keulleobe kwinka /
    kingkadeul mani isseoyo?
*geu keul-luhb-ay kwin-kah /
    king-kahdeul mahnee
    eess-uh-yo?*
그 클럽에 퀸카 / 킹카들
많이 있어요?

**Do you have a
    special room?**

teuksil isseoyo?
teuk-shill eessuh-yo?
특실 있어요?

**Where do you want
    to sit?**

eodie anjeusillaeyo?
uh-dee-ay ahnjeu-shill-lay-yo?
어디에 앉으실래요?

**Let's sit close to the
    dance floor /
    restrooms / exit /
    aisle.**

daenseu peulloeo /
    hwajangsil / chulipgu /
    tongno jjoge gakkapge
    anjeulkkayo?
*dahn-seu-peul-loh-uh / hwah-
    jahng-shill / chooleep-gu /
    tohng-noh chohgay gah-
    kkapgay ahnjeul-kkah-yo?*
댄스 플로어 / 화장실 /
    출입구 / 통로 쪽에
    가깝게 앉을까요?

It's noisy here.

yeogi sikkeureopneyo.
*yawgee shee-kkeu-ruhp-
nay-yo.*
여기 시끄럽네요.

It's too noisy here.

yeogi neomu sikkeureop-
neyo.
*yawgee nuhmoo shee-kkeu-
ruhp-nay-yo.*
여기 너무 시끄럽네요.

**There are too many
people here.**

yeogi sarami neomu
manneyo.
*yawgee sahrahmee nuhmoo
mahnnay-yo.*
여기 사람이 너무 많네요.

It's dark over there.

jeogineun eoduwoyo.
*jaw-gee-neun uh-doo-wah-
yoh.*
저기는 어두워요.

**These seats look
good.**

i jariga johketneyo.
*ee jah-ree-gah choh-ken-
nay-yo.*
이 자리가 좋겠네요.

**Let's move to a
bigger table.**

deo keun teibeullo
olmgilggayo?
*duh keun tay-eebeul-lo
ohlm-gill-kkah-yo?*
더 큰 테이블로
옮길까요?

We need another chair.

uija hana deo pilyohaeyo.
eu-ee-jah hahnah duh peel-yo-hay-yo.
의자 하나 더 필요해요.

I'll get that one over there.

jega jeogi itneun geo hana gajyeo olgeyo.
jay-gah juhgee een-neun guh hanah gahjyaw ohlgay-yo.
제가 저기 있는 거 하나 가져 올게요.

Is instant matching available here?
[To a waiter]

yeogi bukinghaedo dwaeyo?
yawgee bookeeng-hay-doh dway-yo?
여기 부킹해도 돼요?

Instant matching service, called **buking** (*booking*)—that is, a waiter setting you up with a blind date—is very common at nightclubs in Korea.

You sit here.

yeogi anjeuseyo.
yawgee ahn-jeu-say-yo.
여기 앉으세요.

I'll sit here.

jeon yeogi anjeulgeyo.
jahn yawgee ahn-jeul-gay-yo.
전 여기 앉을게요.

Sit by me.

nae yeope anjeuseyo.
nay yawpay ahn-jeu-say-yo.
내 옆에 앉으세요.

Let's pair off.

uri keopeulkkiri
jjijeojyeoyo.
*ooree kuh-peul-ggee-ree
jjee-juh-jyaw-yo.*
우리 커플끼리 찢어져요.

The next two phrases are things you might say to a friend, about a person you see and are planning to approach:

I'm going to get her / him. Don't even touch her / him.

jeo yeoja / namja naega jji-
geosseo. jeo yeoja / namja
nundok deuliji ma.
*jaw yawja / nahmjah naygah
jjeeguss-aw. jaw yawjah /
nahmjah noondohk deul-
ee-jee mah.*
저 여자 / 남자 내가
찍었어. 저 여자 /
남자 눈독 들이지 마.

I'll work on her / him.

jeo yeoja / namja naega
jageop deuleoganda.
*jaw yawja / nahmjah naygah
jahg-up deul-uh-gahn-dah.*
저 여자 / 남자 내가 작업
들어간다.

Will you dance with me?

jeohago chum chusillaeyo?
*jawhah-goh choom choo-shill-
lay-yo?*
저하고 춤 추실래요?

I like to watch you dance.	(geu-nyang) ___ ssi chuneun geo gugyeong hallaeyo. *(geu-nyahng) ___ sshee choo-neun guh goo-gyawng hahllay-yo.* (그냥) ___씨 추는 거 구경할래요.

Start the sentence with the person's name, followed by the suffix **-ssi**.

I'm not good at dancing.	chum jal mot chwoyo. *choom jahl moht chwah-yo.* 춤 잘 못 춰요.

Are you having fun?	jaemi isseoyo? *jehm-ee eessuh-yo?* 재미 있어요?

Yes.	**ne.** (more formal) / **eung.** (less formal) *nay. / eung.* 네. / 응.

Use the first option with a person older than you or whom you don't know well. Choose the second when talking to a friend.

Not really.	byeolloyeyo. *byull-loh-yay-yo.* 별로예요.

I don't feel like dancing yet.	ajik chum chugo sipji anhayo. *ahjeek choom choogoh shipjee ahn-ah-yo.* 아직 춤추고 싶지 않아요.

I'm not going to dance yet.

ajik chum an chul geoyeyo.
ahjeek choom ahn chool guh-yay-yo.
아직 춤 안 출 거예요.

I can't dance to this music.

i eumageneun chumeul chul suga eopseoyo.
ee eumahg-ay-neun choom-eul chool soogah up-suh-yo.
이 음악에는 춤을 출 수가 없어요.

I don't know this song.

i norae mollayo.
ee noh-ray mohl-lah-yo.
이 노래 몰라요.

I like rock 'n' roll.

jeon rak eumakeul joahaeyo.
jawn rock eu-mahg-eul choh-ah-hay-yo.
전 락 음악을 좋아해요.

I like jazz.

jeon jaejeureul joahaeyo.
jawn ja-jeu-reul choh-ah-hay-yo.
전 재즈를 좋아해요.

I like Korean pop music.

jeon hanguk gayoreul joahaeyo.
jawn hahngook ga-hyo-reul choh-ah-hay-yo.
전 한국 가요를 좋아해요.

The dance-floor lights are cool.

jomyeong juginda!
choh-myuhng joogeenda!
조명 죽인다~!

Dancing makes me hot.

chum chunikka deopneyo.
choom choo-nee-kkah duhm-nay-yo.
춤 추니까 덥네요.

Let's get some fresh air.

baram ssoereo gayo.
bahrahm ssway-ruh gah-yo.
바람 쐬러 가요.

What time do they close?

eonje mun dadayo?
awnjay moon dahdah-yo?
언제 문 닫아요?

What time is the last bus?

beoseu makchaga myeotsieyo?
buh-seuh mahk-chah-gah myawtshee-yay-yo?
버스 막차가 몇시에요?

What time do you have to be at work?

myeot sikkaji chulgeun haeya dwaeyo?
myawt shee-kkah-jee chool-geunhay-ya dweh-say-yo?
몇 시까지 출근해야 되세요?

What time is your curfew?

myeot sikkaji deuleoga bwaya dwaeyo? or tonggeumsigani myeotsieyo?

myawt sheekkahjee deul-uh-gah bwahya dweh-yo? or tohng-geum-shee-gah-nee myawt-shee-yay-yo?

몇 시까지 들어가 봐야 되세요? or 통금시간이 몇시에요?

We'll never make it.

an doel geot gatayo.

ahn dwel guht gahtah-yo.

안 될 것 같아요.

It's already too late.

imi neomu neujeosseoyo.

eemee nuhmoo neu-jyuss-uh-yo.

이미 너무 늦었어요.

We've got time.

sigan isseoyo.

sheegahn eessuh-yo.

시간 있어요.

Let's stay to the end.

uri kkeutkkaji namayo.

ooree kkeut-kkah-jee nahmahyo.

우리 끝까지 남아요.

Let's stay till they throw us out.

nagarago hal ttaekkaji
    namaseo nolayo.
*nahgahrahgoh hahl ttay-kkah-
    jee nahmahssuh nohl-ah-yo.*
나가라고 할 때까지
    남아서 놀아요.

Let's go to a café later.

uri najung-e kkapena han
    beon galleyo.
*ooree nahjoong-ay kkah-pay-
    nah hahn buhn gah-lay-yo.*
우리 나중에 카페나 한 번
    갈래요.

May I see you again?

daeume tto bol su
    itsseul-kkayo?
*dah-eum-ay tto bohl soo
    eesseul-kkah-yo?*
다음에 또 볼 수
    있을까요?

Can I have your number?

jeonhwabeonhoreul chom
    allyeo juseyo.
*juhn-hwah-buhn-hoh-reul
    chohm ahl-lyuh joo-say-yo.*
전화번호를 좀 알려
    주세요.

My phone number is... .

jae jeonhwabeonhoneun ... .
*jay juhn-hwah-buhn-hoh-
    neun ... .*
제 전화번호는 … .

6

Sweet Talk

I had a great time yesterday / last night / last week / last Friday.

eoje / jinan bam / jinan ju / jinan geumnyoil jinjja jaemiisseosseoyo.

awjay / jeenahn bahm / jeenahn joo / jeenahn geumyo-eel jeenjjah jehm-eessuh-ssuh-yo.

어제 / 지난 밤 / 지난 주 / 지난 금요일 진짜 재미있었어요.

I couldn't agree with you more.

nae mali!

nay mahlee!

내 말이~!

I think of you night and day.

___ ssi bamnajeuro saenggak haesseoyo.

___ sshee bahm-nah-jeuh-roh sayng-gahk hess-uh-yo.

___ 씨 밤낮으로 생각했어요.

Here, and in many other phrases in this chapter, remember to start the sentence with the person's name, followed by the suffix **-ssi**. Korean people tend not to call someone "you" or say "your" unless the person is close enough. Instead, they use his / her name with **-ssi**.

I couldn't stop thinking about you.	____ ssi saenggagi meomchuji anhayo. _____ sshee saynggahgee muhm-choojee ahnahyo._ ____ 씨 생각이 멈추지 않아요.

Start the sentence with the person's name, followed by the suffix **-ssi**.

I remember what you said.	____ ssi-ga museun mal haet-neunji gieok haeyo. _____ sshee-ga mooseun mahl heht-neun-jee gee-uhk hay-yo._ ____ 씨가 무슨 말했는지 기억해요.

Start the sentence with the person's name, followed by the suffix **-ssi**.

I wanted to call you sooner.	deo iljjik jeonhwa hago sipeosseoyo. _duh eeljjeek juhnhwah hah-goh ship-uhssuh-yo._ 더 일찍 전화하고 싶었어요.

What would you like to do tonight?	oneul bam mwohago sipeuseyo? *oh-neul bahm mwo-hah-goh ship-euh-say-yo?* 오늘 밤 뭐하고 싶으세요?
What sounds good?	mwoga joeulkkayo? *mwohgah choh-eul-kkahyo?* 뭐가 좋을까요?
Do you cook often?	yori jaju haseyo? *yoh-ree jahjoo hay-say-yo?* 요리 자주 하세요?
We could cook dinner together.	uri jeonyeok gati mandeuleo meogeoyo. *ooree juh-nyuhk gahchee mahn-deul-uh maw-guh-yo.* 우리 저녁 같이 만들어 먹어요.
What's your best dish?	museun eumsikeul jeil jal haseyo? *mooseun eumsheek-eul je-eel jahlhay-say-yo?* 무슨 음식을 제일 잘하세요?
I want to try that.	na geugeo hae bollaeyo. *nah geuguh hae bohl-lay-yo.* 나 그거 해볼래요.

Can we meet tomorrow?	**naeil mannal su isseulkkayo?** *nay-eel mahn-nahl soo eesseul-kkayo?* 내일 만날 수 있을까요?
Can you go out this Saturday?	**ibeon ju toyoil naol su isseoyo?** *eebuhn joo toh-yo-eel nah-ohl soo eessuh-yo?* 이번 주 토요일 나올 수 있어요?
I can't wait till then.	**geu ttae kkajineun mot gidarineunde.** *geu ttay kkah-jee-neun moht gee-dah-ree-neun-de.* 그 때까지는 못 기다리는데…
I can wait till then.	**geu ttae kkaji gidaril su it-seoyo.** *geu ttay kkahjee gee-dah-reel soo eessuh-yo.* 그 때까지 기다릴 수 있어요.
I wanna hold your hand.	**son japgo sipeoyo.** *sohn jahpgoh ship-uh-yo.* 손 잡고 싶어요.
Kiss me.	**kiseuhae juseyo.** *kee-seuh-hay joo-say-yo.* 키스해 주세요.

Kiss me deeply.

gipge kiseuhae juseyo.
geepgay keeseu-hay joo-say-yo.
깊게 키스해 주세요.

I want to kiss you.

kiseu hago sipeoyo.
keeseu hah-goh ship-uh-yo.
키스하고 싶어요.

You're a good kisser.

kiseu jal haneyo.
keeseu jahl hahnay-yo.
키스 잘 하네요.

Your lips are so soft.

ipsuli cham budeureopneyo
eepsool-ee chahm boo-deu-ruhm-nay-yo.
입술이 참 부드럽네요.

You're the only one I want.

nahanten neobakke eopseoyo.
nah-hahn-ten naw-bahk-ay up-saw-yo.
나한텐 너밖에 없어요.

I can't live without you / your love.

neo / ni sarang eopsin mot-salayo.
naw / nee sahrahng up-shin moht-sah-lah-yo.
너 / 니 사랑 없인 못살아요.

I'll make you happy.

naega haengbok hage hae
  julgeyo.
naygah hayngbawk hahgay
  hay joolgay-yo.
내가 행복하게 해 줄게요.

**I've never felt this
way before.**

ireon gamjeong cheoeum
  ieyo.
ee-ruhn gahmjuhng chaw-eum
  ee-ay-yo.
이런 감정 처음이에요.

**We had fun together,
didn't we?**

uri jaemiseotjyo, geuchyo?
ooree jehm-iss-ut-jyo,
  geuhchyo?
우리 재미있었죠, 그쵸?

**Do you remember
our first date?**

uri cheot deiteu gieok
  haseyo?
ooree chuht deh-ee-teu
  gee-uhk hah-say-yo?
우리 첫 데이트
  기억하세요?

Look into my eyes.

nae nuneul boseyo.
nay nooneul boh-say-yo.
내 눈을 보세요.

**Stay just a little
bit longer.**

jogeum deo itda gaseyo.
chohgeum duh eetda gah-
  say-yo.
조금 더 있다 가세요.

Stay with me tonight.

oneul bam nahago gati
　　isseoyo.
oh-neul bahm nahhahgo gah-
　　chi eessuh-yo.
오늘 밤 나하고 같이
　　있어요.

**I'll tell you something
—I love you.**

jeon hal mal isseoyo. sarang
　　haeyo.
jawn hahl mahl eessuh-yo.
　　sah-rahng hay-yo.
전 할 말 있어요.
　　사랑해요.

**I know what's on
your mind.**

____ ssi-ga museun saenggak
　　haneunji alayo.
____ sshee-gah mooseun
　　saynggahk hahneun-jee
　　ahlahyo.
____ 씨가 무슨 생각하는지
　　알아요.

Start the sentence with the person's name, followed by the suffix
-ssi.

**You're the only
one I love.**

nae sarangeun dangsin
　　ppuni-eyo.
nay sahrahng-eun dahngsheen
　　ppoon-ee-ay-yo.
내 사랑은 당신 뿐이에요.

I don't love anyone else.

dareun eotteon saramdo sarang haji anhayo.

dahreun aw-ttuhn sahrahm-doh sahrahng hahjee ahnahyo.

다른 어떤 사람도 사랑하지 않아요.

I love you so much I could die.

jugeulmankeum sarang haeyo.

joo-geul-mahn-keum sahrahng hay-yo.

죽을만큼 사랑해요.

I love you for who you are.

dangsin moseup geudaero sarang haeyo.

dahngsheen moh-seup geuhdeh-roh sahrahng hay-yo.

당신 모습 그대로 사랑해요.

Now is the right time.

jigeumi jeil joeun sigiyeyo.

chig-eum-ee jay-eel choh-eun shee-gee-yay-yo.

지금이 제일 좋은 시기예요.

Hold me tight.

nareul kkwak jabeuseyo.

nahreul kkwahk jahb-eu-say-yo.

나를 꽉 잡으세요.

I don't want to go home tonight.

oneul jibe gagi silheoyo.
oh-neul jeep-ay gahgee shill-uh-yo.
오늘 집에 가기 싫어요.

Do you want to come to my place?

uri jibe gallaeyo?
ooree jeep-ay gahl-lay-yo?
우리 집에 갈래요?

I don't want to be used.

i-yong danghago sipji anhayo.
ee-yohng dahng-hah-goh ship-jee ahnahyo.
이용당하고 싶지 않아요.

Trust me.

nal mideoyo.
nahl mee-duh-yo.
날 믿어요.

I want to know all about you.

dangsine daehae modeun geol algo sipeoyo.
dahngsheen-ay daehay moh-deun gull ahlgoh ship-uh-yo.
당신에 대해 모든 걸 알고 싶어요.

You're so very precious.

dangsineun jeongmal sojung haeyo.
dahngsheen-eun jawng-mahl soh-joong hay-yo.
당신은 정말 소중해요.

7

Love and Marriage

Since by now the two of you are getting pretty serious, you probably shouldn't be using formal expressions any more. All the expressions in this chapter are in the casual speech form. If you do want to keep things formal, you can usually just use the sentences below and end them with "**yo**."

When do you want to get married?	eonje gyeolhon hago sipeo? *awnjay gyull-hohn hah-goh ship-aw?* 언제 결혼하고 싶어?
At what age do you want to get married?	myeot sare gyeolhon hago sipeo? *myawt sah-ray gyull-hohn hah-goh ship-aw?* 몇 살에 결혼하고 싶어?

Are you going to work after you're married?

gyeolhon hago naseodo il gye-sok hal geoya?

gyull-hohn hah-goh nah-suh-doh eel gyay-sohk hahl guh-ya?

결혼하고 나서도 일 계속 할 거야?

Do you think you're ready to get married?

gyeolhon hal junbiga dwae isseo?

gyull-hohn-hahl joonbee-gah dway eessaw?

결혼 할 준비가 돼 있어?

Why all these questions about marriage?

wae gyeolhon-e daehaeseo man muleo bwa?

way gyull-hohn-ay day-hay-saw mahn moo-luh bwah?

왜 결혼에 대해서만 물어봐?

Stop beating around the bush!

bing~bing dolliji malgo, geun-yang yaegi hae!

bing-bing dohl-leejee mahl-goh, geun-yahng yay-gee hay!

빙~빙 돌리지 말고, 그냥 얘기해!

Are you trying to propose to me?

jeohante peuropojeu hallyeo-gu?

nah-hahn-tay peuh-roh-poh-jeu hahl-lyaw-goo?

나한테 프로포즈 할려구?

What's the question?	jilmuni mwoji? *jill-moonee mwoh-jee?* 질문이 뭐지?
What's the answer?	daedabi mwoji? *daydahbee mwoh-jee?* 대답이 뭐지?
What's on your mind?	museun saenggak hae? *mooseun saynggahk hay?* 무슨 생각해?
Will you marry me?	jeohago gyeolhon-hae jullaeyo? *jaw-hah-goh gyull-hohn-hay joollay?* 저하고 결혼해 줄래?

Below are not one, but four other Korean ways to ask the all-important question "Will you marry me?"

Will you sleep under the same blanket as me?	jeohago han ibul deopgo sal-lae? *jawhah-goh hahn ee-bool duhp-goh sahl-lay?* 저하고 한 이불 덮고 살래?
Will you wake up every morning with me?	maeil achim jeohago gati ileonallae? *may-eel ahcheem jaw-hah-goh gahchee eel-uh-nahl-lay?* 매일 아침 저하고 같이 일어날래?

Shall we share the rest of our lives together?

uri apeuro pyeongsaeng gachi sallae?

ooree ahpeuhroh pyawng-sayng gahchee sahl-lay?

우리 앞으로 평생 같이 살래?

Will you have my baby?

nae areul naa do! (humorous and informal) / nae aireul na-a jwo! (normal)

nay ah-reul nah-ah doh! / nay ah-ee-reul nah-ah jwah!

내 아를 낳아 도~! / 내 아이를 낳아 줘~!

I can't marry you.

neohago gyeolhon hal sue eopseo.

naw-hah-goh gyull-hohn hahl sso up-so.

너하고 결혼 할 수 없어.

I don't want to marry you.

neohago gyeolhon hago sipji anha.

naw-hah-goh gyull-hohn hah goh shipjee ahnah.

너하고 결혼 하고 싶지 않아.

I can't get married now.

nan jigeum gyeolhonhal su eopseo.

nahn chig-eum gyull-hohn-hahl su up-so.

난 지금 결혼할 수 없어.

Why not?

wae andwaeyo?
way ahn-dway-yo?
왜 안돼요?

Let's get married.

gyeolhon haja. /
    gyeolhon hapsida.
gyull-hohn hahjah. /
    gyull-hohn hahpseedah.
결혼 하자. / 결혼 합시다.

The first option is a more casual and informal way to propose; the
second option is very formal.

**What are you going
    to do about your
    job / school?**

jikjang / hakgyo eotteoke
    hal geoya?
jeek-jahng / hahk-gyoh uh-
    ttuh-kay hahl guh-ya?
직장 / 학교 어떻게 할
    거야?

Are you going to quit work / school?

jikjang / hakgyo geuman dul geoya?

jeek-jahng / hahk-gyoh geum-ahn dool guh-ya?

직장 / 학교 그만 둘 거야?

I should get a better paying job.

yeonbong / wolgeup deo june-un jikjangeul alabwaya hae.

yawnbohng / wolgeup duh joo-neun jeek-jahng-eul ah-lah-bwah-yah hay.

연봉 / 월급 더 주는 직장을 알아봐야 해.

These two sentences convey the same ultimate meaning; the first option 연봉 simply means "annual salary," whereas the second option 월급 means "monthly salary."

I'd better get a second job.

bueobeul haneun ge natgesseo.

boo-uhb-eul hahneun gay nahtgess-uh.

부업을 하는 게 낫겠어.

I don't want my wife to work.

waipeuga il anhaesseumyeon jokesseo.

wah-ee-peu-gah eel ahn-hess-euh-myuhn choh-kessuh.

와이프가 일 안했으면 좋겠어.

I'm sure the neighbors will talk about us.

juwieseo urie daehae yaegi hal geoya.

joo-wee-ay-saw oo-ri-ay day-hay yay-gee hahl guh-ya.

주위에서 우리에 대해 얘기할 거야.

Are you worried about what your neighbors might say?

juwieseo mworago haneun ge singyeong sseo?

joo-wee-ay-saw mwo-rah-goh hah-neun gull shin-gyuhng ssaw?

주위에서 뭐라고 하는 걸 신경써?

Does your family care what the neighbors say?

___ sikgudeureun name nun singyeong sseoyo?

___ sheek-goo-deu-reun nah-may noon shin-gyuhng ssaw?

___ 식구들은 남의 눈 신경 써?

What will your parents think?

___ bumonim kkeseo eo-tteoke saenggak hasil kka?

___ boo-moh-neem kkay-saw uh-ttuh-kay sayng-gahk hah-shill kkah?

___ 부모님께서 어떻게 생각하실까?

**I've already told
my parents.**

beolsseo bumonim kke
    mal-sseum deuryeosseo.
*bawl-saw boo-moh-neem kkay
    mahl-sseum deu-ryuss-aw.*
벌써 부모님께 말씀
    드렸어.

What did they say?

mworago hasideonga?
*mwo-rah-goh hah-shee-
    duhn-gah?*
뭐라고 하시던가?

**Are your parents on
our side?**

___ bumonimeun uri
    pyeoniya?
*___ boo-moh-neem-eun
    ooree pyawn-ee-ya?*
___ 부모님은 우리
    편이야?

**Will your parents
help us?**

___ bumonim kkeseo uril
    dowa jusilkka?
*___ boo-moh-neem kkay-saw
    ooreel doh-wah joo-shill-
    kkah?*
___ 부모님이 우릴 도와
    주실까?

We can live with my parents for a while.	bumonim hago jamkkan dong-an gati sal sudo isseo.
	boo-moh-neem hah-goh jahm-kkahn dohng-ahn gahchee sahl soo-doh eessuh.
	부모님하고 잠깐동안 같이 살 수도 있어.
How long is "a while"?	"jamkkan"-i eoneu jeongdon de?
	"jahm-kkahn"-ee aw-neuh juhng-dohn day?
	"잠깐"이 어느 정돈데?
I should talk to your parents (about it).	___ bumonim hago (i munjee daehaeseo) iyagi hae bwaya gesseo.
	___ boo-moh-neem hah goh (ee moon-jay-ay day-hay-saw) ee yah gee hay bwah-ya gess-aw.
	___ 부모님하고 (이 문제에 대해서) 이야기 해 봐야겠어.
Let me meet your parents.	___ bumonim mannage hae jwo.
	___ boo-moh-neem mahn-nah-gay hay jwah.
	___ 부모님 만나게 해줘.

**Introduce me to
your family.**

nal ___ gajok hante sogae
   sikyeo jwo.

*nahl ___ gah-johk hahn-tay
   soh-gay sheekyaw jwah.*

날 ___ 가족한테 소개시켜
   줘.

**When should I meet
your parents?**

eonje ___ bumonimeul
   manna boeya halkka?

*awnjay ___ boo-moh-neem-
   eul mahnnah bway-yah
   hahl kkah?*

언제 ___ 부모님을 만나
   뵈야 할까?

**I'll meet your parents
as soon as possible.**

___ bumonimeul ganeung-
   han ppalli mannal
   geoya.

*___ boo-moh-neem-eul
   gah-neung-hahn ppahl-lee
   mahnnahl guh-ya.*

___ 부모님을 가능한 빨리
   만날 거야.

**Now is as good a time
as any.**

jigeum-i jeil jo-eun taiming
   iya.

*chig-eum-ee jay-eel choh-eun
   tah-ee-meeng ee-ya.*

지금이 제일 좋은 타이
   밍이야.

**Now is not a good
time.**

jigeum-eun sigiga jochi
   anha.

*chig-eum-eun sheegeegah
   choh-chee ah-nah.*

지금은 시기가 좋지 않아.

Maybe I shouldn't meet your parents now.

jigeum-eun ___ bumonimeul an mannaneun ge jokesseoyo.

chig-eum-eun ___ boo-moh-neem-eul ahn mahn-nah-neun gay chohkesso.

지금은 ___ 부모님을 안 만나는 게 좋겠어.

Maybe some other time.

najung-e.

nahjoong-ay.

나중에.

We can do it later.

uri geugeo najung-e hae.

ooree geuguh nahjoong-ay hay.

우리 그거 나중에 해.

Do you think your parents will accept our marriage?

___ bumonim kkeseo uri gyeolhoneul heorak hasil kka?

___ boo-moh-neem-kkay-saw ooree gyull-hohn-eul haw-rahk hahshill kkah?

___ 씨 부모님께서 우리 결혼을 허락하실까?

Tell me what to do in front of your family.

___ gajok apeseo eotteoke haeya haneunji gareuchyeo jwo.

___ gah-johk ahp-ay-saw uh-ttuh-kay hayah hah-neun-jee gah-reuh-chyaw jwah.

___ 가족 앞에서 어떻게 해야 하는지 가르쳐 줘.

What should I talk about?	naega museun maleul haeya haji? *nay-gah mooseun mahleul hay-ah hah-jee?* 내가 무슨 말을 해야 하지?
What shall I / we bring?	mwol deulgo gaya dwae? *mwol deul-goh gah-yah dway?* 뭘 들고 가야 돼?
Tell me what to say.	museun yaegireul haeya doeneunji gareuchyeo jwah. *mooseun yay-gee-reul hay-ah dway-neunjee gah-reuh-chyaw jwah.* 무슨 얘기를 해야 되는지 가르쳐 줘.
Do you think your family will like me?	___ gajogi nal joahal-kka? *___ gah-johg-ee nahl choh-ah-hahl-kkah?* ___ 가족이 날 좋아할까?
Does your father smoke?	abeonimi dambae piwo? *ah-buh-neem-ee dahm-bay pee-wah?* 아버님이 담배 피워?
Does your father drink?	abeonimi suleul deusyeo? *ah-buh-neem-ee sool-eul deu-shaw?* 아버님이 술을 드셔?

What's your father's hobby / work?	abeonim chwimiga / jigeob-i mwoya? *ah-buh-neem chwee-mee-gah / jeeg-up-ee mwo-yay?* 아버님 취미가 / 직업이 뭐야?
What's your mother's hobby / work?	omeonim chwimiga / jigeob-i mwoyeyo? *aw-muh-neem chwee-mee-gah / jeeg-up-ee mwo-yay-yo?* 어머님 취미가 / 직업이 뭐야?

A few conversation-starting phrases that can be useful when meeting the relatives. All the sentences below are in polite speech.

Where are you from?	eodi chulsin iyeyo? *uh-dee choolsheen ee-yay-yo?* 어디 출신이에요?
Ah yes, I've been there.	a, ne. geogi ga bon jeoki isseoyo. *ah, nay. guh-gee gah bohn juhg-ee eessuh-yo.* 아, 네. 거기 가 본 적이 있어요.
Have you ever been to...?	... e ga bonjeoki isseoyo? *... ay gah bohn juhg-ee iss-uh-yo?* ⋯ 에 가 본적이 있어요?

Who might oppose our marriage?

uri gyeolhoneul nuga
   bandae halkkayo?
*ooree gyull-hohn-eul noogah
   bahn-day hahl-kkah-yoh?*
우리 결혼을 누가
   반대할까요?

Who will support our marriage?

uri gyeolhoneul nuga chan-
   seong halkkayo?
*ooree gyull-hohn-eul noogah
   chahn-suhng hahl-kkah-
   yoh?*
우리 결혼을 누가
   찬성할까요?

How much will the wedding cost?

gyeolhon biyong-i eolmana
   doelkkayo?
*gyull-hohn bee-yohng-ee ull-
   mah-nah dwel-kkah-yoh?*
결혼 비용이 얼마나
   될까요?

We have to hurry to have the wedding.

gyeolhon haryeomyeon
   seodulleoya haeyo.
*gyull-hohn hah-ryaw-myuhn
   saw-dool-luh-yah hay-yo.*
결혼하려면 서둘러야
   해요.

We should begin preparing now.

jigeum junbireul haeya
   haeyo.
*chig-eum joonbee-reul
   hay-yah hay-yo.*
지금 준비를 해야 해요.

Should we have a Korean or a Western-style wedding?

hanguk jeontong hollyero halkkayo, geunyang yesikjangeseo halkkayo?

hahngook juhn-tohng hohl-lyay-roh hahl-kkah-yo, geu-nyahng yay-sheek-jahng-ay-saw hahl-kkah-yoh?

한국 전통 혼례로 할까요, 그냥 예식장에서 할까요?

What's the difference?

chaijeom-i mwoyeyo?

chah-ee-juhm-ee mwo-yay-yo?

차이점이 뭐예요?

I run three kilometers every day.
Maeil sam killo-ssik dallyeoyo.

I go to the health club.
Helseu keulleobe danyeoyo.

I play tennis.
Teniseu haeyo.

Did you gain weight?
Sal jjyeosseoyo?

8

Health

You have a nice figure.	mommaega joeusineyo. *mohm-may-gah choh-euh-* *shee-nay-yo.* 몸매가 좋으시네요.
You're slim.	nalssin hasineyo. *nahl-ssheen hah-shee-nay-yo.* 날씬하시네요.
Did you lose weight?	sal ppaesseoyo? *sahl ppehssuh-yo?* 살 뺐어요?
Did you gain weight?	sal jjyeosseoyo? *sahl jjyawssuh-yo?* 살 쪘어요?

Do you think I need to diet?

jeo daieoteu haeya doel geot gatayo?
jaw dah-ee-uh-teuh hay-yah dwel guht gahtah-yo?
저 다이어트해야 될 것 같아요?

No, I like the way you are now.

aniyo, jigeum geudaeroga joayo.
ah-neeyo, chig-eum geuh-day-roh-gah choh-ah-yo.
아니요, 지금 그대로가 좋아요.

Maybe you could try dieting.

daieoteu haeya hal geot gatneyo.
dah-ee-uh-teuh hay-yah hahl guht gahn-nay-yoh.
다이어트 해야 할 것 같네요.

You need to go on a diet.

daieoteu haeya dwaeyo.
dah-ee-uh-teuh hay-ya dway-yo.
다이어트 해야 돼요.

I'm on a diet now.

jigeum daieoteu jung-ieyo.
chig-eum dah-ee-uh-teuh joongee-ay-yo.
지금 다이어트 중이에요.

Diets (and well-being; see below) are extremely popular in Korea, where people (both men and women) tend to put a lot of effort into their appearance.

I don't eat fried food.

twigin eumsigeun an meogeoyo.
twigeen eum-sheeg-eun ahn maw-guh-yo.
튀긴 음식은 안 먹어요.

I try not to eat sweet food (as much as I can).

doel su it-seumyeon dan eumsigeun an meogeuryeoguyo.
dwel soo eess-euh-myuhn dahn eum-sheeg-eun ahn maw-geu-ryaw-goo-yo.
될 수 있으면 단 음식은 안 먹으려구요.

I can't live without McDonalds!

maekdonaldeu eopseumyeon mot salayo!
mack-daw-nahl-deu up-seu-myuhn moht sah-lah-yo!
맥도날드 없으면 못 살아요~!

In spite of the dieting / well-being trend and emphasis on appearance, both Korean and Western fast food chains are ubiquitous in Korea. The menu items are often a little different (for example, *bulgogi* burgers, or burgers with rice used to make the buns) but still pretty unhealthy. McDonald's, KFC, Baskin Robbins, Subway, and various pizza places are not at all hard to find in any city of any size.

I don't have time to cook proper meals.

yorihal sigani eopseoyo.
yoh-ree-hahl sheegah-nee up-suh-yo.
요리할 시간이 없어요.

I know some healthy restaurants.

welbing sikdangeul myeot gunde alayo.
wel-beeng sheekdahng-eul myawt goon-day ah-lah-yo.
웰빙 식당을 몇 군데 알아요.

You should eat fewer snacks.

gwajareul jogeumman meogeoya dwaeyo.
gwah-jah-reul choh-geum-mahn maw-gaw-yah dway-yo.
과자를 조금만 먹어야 돼요.

You shouldn't drink so much beer.

maekjureul geureoke mani masimyeon an dwaeyo.
meck-joo-reul geu-ruh-kay mah-nee mah-shee-myuhn ahn dway-yo.
맥주를 그렇게 많이 마시면 안 돼요.

You should stop smoking.	dambaereul kkeuneoya dwaeyo. *dahmbay-reul kkeu-nuh-yah dway-yo.* 담배를 끊어야 돼요.
Stop smoking.	dambae kkeuneuseyo. *dahmbay kkeu-neuh-say-yo.* 담배 끊으세요.
Smoking is bad for your health.	dambaeneun geongange haerowoyo. *dahmbay-neun guhn-gahng-ay hay-roh-wah-yo.* 담배는 건강에 해로워요.
You need to exercise.	undong hasyeoya hal geot gatayo. *oondohng hah-syaw-yah hahl guht kah-tah-yo.* 운동하셔야 할 것 같아요.
Do you exercise?	undong haseyo? *oondohng hah-say-yo?* 운동하세요?
Do you like to exercise?	undong joahaseyo? *oondohng choh-ah-hah-say-yo?* 운동 좋아하세요?
We can do it together.	uri gachi haeyo. *ooree gahchee hay-yo.* 우리 같이 해요.

What type of exercise do you do?

eotteon undong haseyo?
aw-ttuhn oondohng hah-say-yo?
어떤 운동 하세요?

I run three kilometers every day.

maeil sam killo-ssik dallyeoyo.
may-eel sahm kill-oh-ssheek dahl-lyaw-yo.
매일 삼 킬로씩 달려요.

I go to the health club.

helseu keulleobe danyeoyo.
helseuh keul-luhb-ay dah-nyaw-yo.
헬스 클럽에 다녀요.

I go to the pool.

suyeongjang danyeoyo.
soo-young-jahng dah-nyaw-yo.
수영장 다녀요.

I like to swim.

suyeongeul joahaeyo.
soo-young-eul choh-ah-hay-yo.
수영을 좋아해요.

I play soccer / tennis / golf.

chukgu / teniseu / golpeu-reul chyeoyo.
chook-goo / the-nee-seu / gol-peuh-reul chyaw-yo.
축구 / 테니스 / 골프-를 쳐요.

I only eat well-being food.

jeoneun welbing
   eumsingman meogeoyo.
*jaw-neun welbeeng eum-
   sheekmahn maw-guh-yo.*
저는 웰빙 음식만 먹어요.

The "well-being" trend is popular in Korea, and the phrase "well-being food" is used in Korean for what English speakers might term "health food." It's often used as a marketing buzzword, and is sometimes used for things that are far from healthy!

Lovers' Arguments

Love in Korea tends to unfold a little differently than in the West. First of all, though Western-style dating is now the norm, matchmaking services and arranged marriages are still pretty common, especially in more rural areas.

Secondly (and probably more relevant to you), compared to Westerners, Koreans generally prefer a lot more closeness than attention in their relationships. Constant text message conversations all day long are often expected, as are little gifts for all the anniversaries (and I do mean ALL the anniversaries—better keep track of exactly how long you've been dating so you don't miss that crucial hundred-day anniversary!).

Then there are Peppero Day, Red Day and White Day (February and March 14th, respectively—girls give presents on Red Day, and men on White Day) and any number of other days that haven't quite caught on to the same extent. Hopefully you can keep track of it all so you don't find yourself needing to look through this chapter again…

This chapter is also written in informal speech. Again, if you're using any of these sentences toward someone you don't know well, in most cases you can get away with just adding 요 (**yo**) to the very end of any sentence here.

It wasn't your day, was it?	**oneul byeollo an joatji, geuji?** *oh-neul byull-oh ahn choh-aht-jee, geu-jee?* 오늘 별로 안 좋았지, 그지?
It's boring, isn't it?	**jigyeopji, geuji?** *jee-gyawp-jee, geu-jee?* 지겹지, 그지?
I don't want you to get hurt on my account.	**na ttaemune sangcheo batji anatsseumyeon jokesseo.** *nah ttay-moon-ay sahng-chuh baht-jee ahnahss-eu-myuhn choh-kessuh.* 나 때문에 상처받지 않았으면 좋겠어.
Do you care what they think?	**namdeuli eotteoke saenggak haneunji singyeong sseo?** *nahm-deu-lee uh-tuh-kkay sayng-gahk hah-neun-jee shin-gyawng ssuh?* 남들이 어떻게 생각하는지 신경써?

Don't let it bother you (what others think).

namdeuli mworadeun
    singyeong sseuji ma.
*nahm-deul-ee mwo-rah-deun
    shin-gyawng sseujee mah.*
남들이 뭐라든 신경쓰지
    마.

Don't be upset.

hwanaeji ma.
hwah-nay-jee mah.
화내지 마.

Does your family know about us?

___ gajogi uri-e daehaeseo
    ala?
*___ gah-johgee ooree-ay
    day-hay-suh ah-lah?*
___ 가족이 우리에 대해서
    알아?

I told my family about you.

uri gajogege ___ yaegi
    haesseo.
*ooree gah-johg-ay-gay ___
    yay-gee hess-aw.*
우리 가족에게 ___ 얘기
    했어.

Tell me, what do you think?

malhaebwa. eotteoke
    saenggak hae?
*mahl-hay-bwah. uh-ttuh-kkay
    sayng-gak hay?*
말해봐. 어떻게 생각해?

Make it clear.

hwaksilhage hae.
hwahk-shill-hah-gay hay.
확실하게 해.

Please don't go.

gaji ma.
gahjee mah.
가지 마.

You don't know.

____ neun molla.
____ nohn moh-lah.
___는 몰라.

We've known each other for three months now.

uri mannanji se dal dwae-sseo.
ooree mahn-nahn-jee say dahl dwess-aw.
우리 만난지 세 달 됐어.

I want to know what you're feeling.

____ gamjeongeul algo sipeo.
____ gahm-juhng-eul ahl-goh ship-aw.
___ 감정을 알고 싶어.

It'll all change.

da bakkwil geoya.
dah bah-kkwil guh-ya.
다 바뀔 거야.

Let's not get serious now.

simgakhage saenggak haji ma.
sheem-gahk-hah-gay sayng-gahk hahjee ma.
심각하게 생각하지 마.

I don't (even) want to think about it.

geugeoneun saenggakdo hagi sileo.
geu-guh-neun sayng-gahk-doh hah-gee shill-aw.
그거는 생각도 하기 싫어.

What does that mean?	**museun tteusia?** *moo-seun tteu-shee-ah?* 무슨 뜻이야?
Don't cry.	**uljima. / ttuk! / ulji maseyo.** *ooljeemah. / ttook! /* *ooljee mah-say-yo.* 울지마. / 뚝! / 울지 마세요.

The first two ways to say "don't cry" are informal. The third way is formal.

Wipe your tears away.	**nunmul dakkayo.** *noon-mool dah-kkah.* 눈물 닦아.
Don't be sad.	**seulpeohaji ma.** *seul-puh-hah-jee mah.* 슬퍼하지 마.
Cheer up.	**him nae.** *him-nay.* 힘내.

**Don't worry;
be happy.**
	geokjeong malgo,
	     pyeonhage saenggak hae.
	guhk-juhng mahl-goh, pyawn-
	hah-ge sayng-gahk hay.
	걱정 말고, 편하게
	     생각해.

Let's talk about this later.	**daeume yaegi hae.** *dah-eum-ay yay-gee hay.* 다음에 얘기해.

Let's change the subject.	dareun yaegi haja. *dah-reun yay-gee hah-jah.* 다른 얘기하자.
By the way...	geureonde... *geu-ruhn-day...* 그런데…
Don't change the subject.	jujereul bakkuji ma. *joo-jay-reul bah-kkoo-jee mah.* 주제를 바꾸지 마.
Please listen to me. / Let me explain.	nae mal jom deuleo bwa. / naega seolmyeong halge. *nay mahl chohm deul-uh bwah. / naygah sull-myuhng hahlgay.* 내 말 좀 들어봐. / 내가 설명할게.
I was only joking.	geunyang nongdam ieosseoyo. *geun-yahng nohng-dahm ee-uss-aw.* 그냥 농담이었어.
Don't take it so seriously.	neomu simgakhage bada deuliji ma. *nuhmoo sheem-gahk-hah-gay bah-dah deul-ee-jee mah.* 너무 심각하게 받아들이지 마.
Don't do that again.	dasin geureoji ma. *dah-sheen geu-ruh-jee mah.* 다신 그러지 마.

I'll forget about it.

geugeon ijeo beorilge.
geu-guhn eejuh baw-reel-gay.
그건 잊어 버릴게.

Are you still mad?

ajikdo hwanasseo?
ahjeek-doh hwah-nahss-aw?
아직도 화났어?

You're still mad, aren't you?

ajikdo hwanatji, geuji?
ahjeek-doh hwah-naht-jee, goh-jee?
아직도 화났지, 그지?

I think I was wrong.

naega jalmothan geot gata.
naygah jahlmoht-hahn guht gahtah.
내가 잘못한 것 같아.

I shouldn't have done that.

geureoji marasseoya haenneunde.
geu-ruh-jee mahrahss-uh-yah hen-neun-day.
그러지 말았어야 했는데.

I don't know why I did that.

naega wae geuraenneunji moreugesseo.
naygah way geuh-rett-neun-jee moh-reu-gess-aw.
내가 왜 그랬는지 모르겠어.

I think I was too excited.

neomu heungbun haesseotna bwa.
nuhmoo heung-boon hess-uht-nah bwah.
너무 흥분했었나 봐.

I think I was too nervous.

neomu yemin haesseotna bwa.

nuhmoo yay-meen hess-uht-nah bwah.

너무 예민했었나 봐.

I was out of my mind.

je jeongsini aniyeosseo.

jay juhng-sheen-ee ah-nee-yuhss-aw.

제 정신이 아니였어.

It was silly of me (to do that).

naega babo yeosseo.

naygah bahboh yuhss-aw.

내가 바보였어.

If you change your mind, let me know.

mam bakkwimyeon allyeo-jwo.

mahm bah-kkwi-myuhn ahl-lyaw-jwah.

맘 바뀌면 알려줘.

What changed your mind?

wae maeumi bakkwi-eosseoyo?

way mah-eum-ee bah-kkwee-uss-uh-yo?

왜 마음이 바뀌었어요?

I didn't mean to hurt you.

___ hante sangcheo-juryeogo hange aninde.

___ hahn-te sahng-chuh-joo-ryaw-goh hahn gay ahn-een-day.

___한테 상처주려고 한게 아닌데.

I should've thought about it more.	deo gipge saeng gakhae bwat-seoya haenneunde. *duh geep-gay sayng-gahk-hay bwahss-uh-yah het-neun-day.* 더 깊게 생각해 봤어야 했는데.
I hurt your feelings, didn't I?	naega sangcheo jwotjyo, geujyo? *nay-gah sahng-chuh jwuht-jee, geu-jee?* 내가 상처줬지, 그지?
I know I hurt your feelings.	naega sangcheo jungeo alayo. *naygah sahng-chuh joon-guh ah-lah.* 내가 상처 준거 알아.
I'll do anything to make you forgive me.	___ i / ga yongseoman hae jundamyeon mwodeunji halgeyo. *___ ee / gah yong-suh-mahn hay joon-dah-myuhn mwo-deunjee hahl-gay.* ___이 / 가 용서만 해 준다면 뭐든지 할게.

No need to delve too deeply into the grammar here, but basically, if your lover's name ends in a vowel sound, use **-ga** (**Sara-ga** 사라가, **Mike-ga** 마이크가) and if it ends in a consonant, use **-i** (**John-i** 존이, **Michelle-i** 미셸이).

Anything?	mwodeunji? *mwoh-deun-jee?* 뭐든지?

I was blind to the truth.

nan saekkamake moreugo it-seotne.

nahn say-kkah-mah-kay moh-reu-goh eess-uht-nay.

난 새까맣게 모르고 있었네.

You should understand how I feel.

nae gamjeong jom ihaehae jwo.

nay gahm-juhng chohm ee-hay-hay jwah.

내 감정 좀 이해해 줘.

You didn't even listen to me.

___ neun nae maleul deu-leuryeogodo haji anasseo.

___ neun nay mah-leul deul-eu-ryaw-goh-doh hah-jee ah-nahss-aw.

___는 내 말을 들으려고도 하지 않았어.

Let's get back together.

dasi yejeoneuro dolagaja.

dahshee yay-juhn-eu-roh dohl-ah-gah-jah.

다시 예전으로 돌아가자.

Promise it will never happen again.

dasineun an geureondago yak-sok hae.

dah-shee-neun ahn geu-ruhn-dah-goh yahk-sohk hay.

다시는 안 그런다고 약속해.

I promise.

yaksok halge.
yahk-sohk hahl-gay.
약속할게.

Please take me back.

yejeoneuro dolagago sipeo.
yay-juhn-eu-roh dohl-ah-gah-
goh ship-aw.
예전으로 돌아가고 싶어.

I'm always doing silly things.

nan hangsang huhoehal
jitman handanikka.
nahn hahng-sahng hoo-hway
hahl jeet-mahn hahn-
dahnee-kkah.
난 항상 후회할 짓만
한다니까.

I feel so lonely.

nan neomu oerowo.
nahn nuhmoo way-roh-wah.
난 너무 외로워.

I'm losing sleep.

jami an wa.
jah-mee ahn wah.
잠이 안 와.

You were the first and you'll be the last.

___ neun nae cheoeumija
majimagia.
___ neun nay chaw-eum-ee-
jah mah-jee-mah-gee-yah.
___ 는 내 처음이자
마지막이야.

Whenever you need someone, I'll always be there.

___ i / ga pilyohal ttaen, eon-jena naega geu gose isseul geoya.

___ ee / gah pill-yoh-hahl ttayn awn-jehn-nah nay-gah geu gohs-ay eesseul-guh-ya.

___ 이 / 가 필요할 땐, 언제나 내가 그 곳에 있을거야.

Whatever you want I'll give it to you.

___ i / ga wonhaneun geol naega da haejulgeoya.

___ ee / gah won-hah-neun gull nay-gah dah hay-jool-guh-yah.

___ 이 / 가 원하는 걸 내가 다 해줄게.

Come back to me.

naegero dolawa.
nay-gay-roh dohl-ah-wah.
내게로 돌아와.

I believe you still love me.

ajikdo nal sarang halgeorago mideo.
ahjeek-doh nahl sah-rahng hahl guh-rah-goh mee-daw.
아직도 날 사랑할거라고 믿어.

Don't throw away this chance.

i gihoereul nochiji ma.
ee gee-hway-reul noh-chee-jee mah.
이 기회를 놓치지 마.

It might be your last.

ige majimagil jido molla.
ee-gay mah-jee-mah-geel jeedoh mohl-law.
이게 마지막일지도 몰라.

10

Even More Things to Argue About

This chapter is also written in informal speech. Again, if you're using any of these sentences toward someone you don't know well, in most cases you can get away with just adding 요 (**yo**) to the very end of any sentence here.

Where did you go?	**eodi gasseo?** *aw-dee gah-saw?* 어디 갔어?
You forget everything.	**___ neun hangsang gieogeul mot-hae.** *___ neun hahng-sahng gee-uhg-eul moht-hay.* ___는 항상 기억을 못해.
Have you forgotten so soon?	**beol-sseo ijeo beoryeosseo?** *bawl-ssuh eejaw buh-ryuss-uh?* 벌써 잊어버렸어?

You forgot my birthday.

nae saengil ijeo meogeot jana.

nay sayng-eel eejyaw mawguht-jahnah.

내 생일 잊어 먹었잖아.

You forgot our anniversary.

uri ginyeomil ijeo meogeot jana.

ooree gee-nyawm-eel eejyaw mawguht-jahnah.

우리 기념일 잊어 먹었잖아.

Are you making fun of me?

nollinya?

nohl-lee-nyah?

놀리냐?

Why didn't you call me?

wae jeonhwa an haesseo?

way juhn-wah ahn hess-uh?

왜 전화 안했어?

I waited all night / a long time for your call.

bamsae ___ jeonhwaman gidaryeosseo.

bahmsay ___ juhn-hwah- mahn gee-dah-ryuss-aw.

밤새 ___ 전화만 기다렸어.

I was just about to call you.

mak jeonhwa haryeodeon chamieosseo.

mahk juhn-hwah hah-ryaw- duhn chahm-ee-uss-aw.

막 전화 하려던 참이었어.

I tried to call you.

jeonhwa haryeogo haesseo.
*juhn-hwah hah-ryaw-goh
    hess-aw.*
전화 하려고 했어.

I was busy.

bappasseo.
bah-ppassuh.
바빴어.

**Why didn't you
email me?**

wae i-meil an haesseoyo?
way ee-may-eel ahn hess-aw?
왜 이메일 안 했어?

**My (phone's) battery
was dead.**

(jeonhwagi) baeteori
    nagat-sseo.
*(juhn-hwah-gee) baht-deh-
    ree-gah nah-gahssuh.*
(전화기) 배터리가
    나갔어.

I was out of range.

tonghwa ganeung jiyeogeul
    beoseonasseo.
*tohng-hwah gah-neung jee-
    yuhg-eul buss-uh-nass-aw.*
통화 가능 지역을
    벗어났어.

Where were you?

eodi isseosseoyo?
uh-dee ees-uss-aw?
어디 있었어?

That's a secret.

bimiriya.
bee-mee-ree-yah.
비밀이야.

Don't trick me / lie to me.	sogiji ma. / geojitmal haji ma. *soh-gee-jee mah. / guh-jeen-mahl hah-jee mah.* 속이지 마. / 거짓말 하지 마.
You lied to me.	___ nahante geojitmal haesseo. *___ nah-hahn-tay guh-jeen-mahl hess-uh.* ___ 나한테 거짓말 했어.
You lie to me all the time.	___ neun hangsang nahante geojitmal hae. *___ neun hahng-sahng nah-hahn-tay guh-jeen-mahl hay.* ___ 는 항상 나한테 거짓말 해.
Stop lying to me.	geojitmal jom geuman hae. *guh-jeen-mahl chohm geu-mahn hay.* 거짓말 좀 그만해.
You're so annoying!	jjajeungna! *jah-jeung-nah!* 짜증나

This can be used any time you're annoyed by something—if the air conditioning is broken, if you have to stay late at work, if there are too many people on your bus…

It was stupid of me to trust you.

___ reul mideun naega baboji.

___ reul meedeun naygah bahboh-jee.

___를 믿은 내가 바보지.

I can't trust you anymore.

___ neun deo isang mot mitgesseo.

___ neun duh eesahng moht meet-gessuh.

___ 는 더 이상 못 믿겠어.

Everything you've said is a lie.

malman hamyeon geojitmali-janha.

mahl-mahn hahmyuhn guh-jeen-mah-lee-jah-nah.

말만하면 거짓말이잖아.

So, what do you want me to say?

geureom, naega museon maleul hae jugil barae?

geu-ruhm, nay-gah moo-seun mahleul hay joogeel bahray?

그럼, 내가 무슨 말을 해 주길 바래?

Let me speak frankly.

soljikhage yaegihalge.

sohl-jeek-hah-gay yay-gee-hahl-gay.

솔직하게 얘기할게.

I'm sorry, but...

mianhajiman...

mee-ahn-hah-jee-mahn...

미안하지만…

Do you want to know the truth?	sasileul (or jinsileul) algo sipeo? *sah-shee-leul (or jin-shee-leul) ahl-goh ship-aw?* 사실을 (or 진실을) 알고 싶어?
What you say isn't important.	___ i / ga museun mareul haenneunjineun jungyo haji anha. *___ ee / gah moo-seun mah-leul han-neun-jee-neun joong-yo hahjee ahnah.* ___ 이 / 가 무슨 말을 했는지는 중요하지 않아.

Again, if your lover's name ends in a vowel sound, use **-ga** (**Sara-ga** 사라가, **Mike-ga** 마이크가) and if it ends in a consonant, use **-i** (**John-i** 존이, **Michelle-i** 미셸이).

You're so selfish!	___ neun neomu igijeogiya. *___ neun nuh-moo ee-gee-juhg-ee-ya.* ___ 는 너무 이기적이야.
Who am I to you?	___ ege nan (dodaeche) mwoji? *___ ay-gay nahn (doh-day-chay) mwoh-jee?* ___ 에게 난 (도대체) 뭐지?

Who do you think I am?	___ neun nal eotteoke saenggak hae? *___ neun nahl uh-tuh-kkay sayng-gahk hay?* ___ 는 날 어떻게 생각해?
I wasn't born yesterday.	naega babon jul ala? *nay-gah bah-bohn jool ah-lah?* 내가 바본 줄 알아?
Don't pretend nothing happened.	amu geotdo anin cheok haji mal. *ahmoo guht-do ahneen chuck hahjee mah.* 아무 것도 아닌 척 하지 말아.
How can you act like that (to me)?	nahante eotteoke ireol su isseo? *nah-hantay uh-tuh-kkay ee-rull soo iss-aw?* 나한테 어떻게 이럴 수 있어?
You made me do it.	___ ttaemune geuraet janha. *___ ttay-moo-nay geu-reht-jahn-ah.* ___ 때문에 그랬잖아.
Don't make excuses.	pinggye daeji ma. *peeng-gyay day-jee mah.* 핑계대지 말아.

11

Breaking Up

Like the preceding two chapters, this one is also written in informal speech. Again, if you're using any of these sentences toward someone you don't know well, in most cases you can get away with just adding 요 (**yo**) to the very end of any sentence here.

You told me that you loved me, didn't you?	nal sarang handago haet janha, aniya? *nahl sahrahng hahn-dah-goh hett-jah-nah, ah-nee-ya?* 날 사랑한다고 했잖아. 아니야?
Are you telling me you don't love me anymore?	nal deo isang sarang haji anneundaneun maliya? *nahl duh eesahng sahrahng hahjee ahn-neun-dah-neun mahl-ee-ya?* 날 더 이상 사랑하지 않는다는 말이야?

I'm tired of you.

___ siljeung nasseo /
jigyeowo.
*___ shill-jeung nahssaw /
jee-gyaw-wah.*
___ 싫증났어 / 지겨워.

Are you tired of me?

nahante siljeung nasseo?
*nah-hahn-tay shill-jeung
nahssuh?*
나한테 싫증났어?

**I knew it wouldn't
work.**

an tonghal jul alasseo.
*ahn tohnghahl jool ah-lahss-
aw.*
안 통할 줄 알았어.

**You've changed,
haven't you?**

___ byeonhaesseo, aninga?
*___ byawn-hess-uh, ah-neen-
gah?*
___ 변했어, 아닌가?

You messed up my life.

___ i / ga nae insaengeul
mangchyeo nwasseo.
*___ ee / gah nay eensang-eul
mahng-chyaw nwahssuh.*
___ 이 / 가 내 인생을
망쳐 놨어.

**Don't hurt me
anymore.**

deo isang nahante sangcheo
juji ma.
*duh eesahng nah-hahn-tay
sahng-chaw joojee mah.*
더 이상 나한테 상처주지
마.

Let's not tie each other up.

ije uri inyeon kkeuneo.
eejay ooree eenyawn kkeuhnuh.
이제 우리 인연 끊어.

You're the one who said, "Let's stop seeing each other."

heeojijago han sarameun ___ ya.
hay-uh-jee-jah-goh hahn sah-rahm-eun ___ya.
헤어지자고 한 사람은 ___ 야.

You're using me.

dangsineun nal iyonghae meogeosseo.
dahngsheen-eun nahl eeyong-hay maw-guss-aw.
당신은 날 이용해 먹었어.

Do you know what you're doing?

dangsini museun jiseul hago itneunji ala?

dahngsheen-ee moo-seun jeeseul hah-goh een-neun-jee ah-lah?

당신이 무슨 짓을 하고 있는지 알아?

Be careful: In English this phrase is understood as neutral or innocuous, but the Korean sentence has a distinctly negative meaning. The Korean 짓 in **jiseul** is used when referring to bad behavior. Thus, the sentence above can literally be translated, "Do you know what kind of (bad) behavior you are doing?"

You take me for granted.

dangsineun nal neomu manman hage saeng-gak hae.

dahngsheen-eun nahl nuhmoo mahn-mahn hahgay sayng-gahk hay.

당신은 날 너무 당연하게 여겼어.

Don't tell me what to do.

nahante iraera jeoraera haji ma.

nah-hahn-tay eeray-rah jaw-ray-rah hahjee mah.

나한테 이래라 저래라 하지 마.

I don't tell you what to do.

____ hante iraera jeoraera haneun geo aniya.

____ hahn-tay eeray-rah jaw-ray-rah hahneun guh ahnee-ya.

____한테 이래라 저래라 하는 거 아니야.

I'll do whatever I want.

naega hago sipeun daero hal geoya.

naygah hah-goh ship-eunday-roh hahl guh-ya.

내가 하고 싶은대로 할 거야.

Don't try to change me.

nal bakkuryeogo haji ma.

nahl bah-kkoo-ryaw-goh hahjee mah.

날 바꾸려고 하지 마.

I can't be what you want me to be.

___ i / ga wonhaneun sarami dwaejul su eopseo.

___ ee / gah won-hah-neun sah-rahmee dway-jool soo up-suh.

___ 이 / 가 원하는 사람이 돼줄 수 없어.

Let me be me.

nal itneun geudaero bwa-jwo.

nahl een-neun geu-day-roh bwah-jwah.

날 있는 그대로 봐줘.

Leave me alone.

nal honja itge naebeoryeo dwo.

nahl hohnjah eetgay nay-buh-ryaw dwah.

날 혼자 있게 내버려 둬.

**Stop following
me around.**

na ttara daniji ma.
nah ttahrah dahneejee mah.
나 따라다니지 마.

**Stop checking up
on me.**

nae dwitjosa jom geuman
hae.
*nay dwit-chohsah chohm
geu-mahn hay.*
내 뒷조사 좀 그만해.

Stop bothering me.

na gwichanke haji ma.
*nah gwee-chahnkay hahjee
mah.*
나 귀찮게 하지 마.

Don't embarrass me.

na jom danghwang
seurepge haji ma.
*nah chohm dahng-hwahng
seu-ruhp-gay hahjee mah.*
나 좀 당황스럽게 하지 마.

Don't disappoint me (again).	(dasineun) nal silmang sikiji ma. *(dahshee-neun) nahl shill-mahng sheekeejee mah.* (다시는) 날 실망시키지 마.
I'm disappointed in you!	___ silmang iya! *___ shil-mahng eeyah!* 실망이야~!
How many girls / men have you made cry?	eolmana maneun yeojareul / namjareul ullyeotji? *ull-mahnah mahneun yawjah-reul / nahm-jah-reul ool-lyawt-jee?* 얼마나 많은 여자를 / 남자를 울렸지?

In this and other sentences, remember that 남자 (**namja**) means man and 여자 (**yeoja**) means woman, and choose accordingly.

Think about the way you acted / treated me!	___ i / ga nahante eotteoke haetneunji saenggakhae bwa. *___ ee / gah nah-hantay uh-ttuh-kay heht-neun-jee sayng-gahk-hay bwah.* ___ 이 / 가 나한테 어떻게 했는지 생각해 봐.
Are you playing around with me?	nal gatgo non geoya? *nahl gat-goh nohn guh-ya?* 날 갖고 논거야?

I didn't mean to.

ilbureo geureoryeogo
   haetdeon geon aniya.
*eel-boo-ruh geu-ruh-ryaw-goh
   heht-duhn guhn
   ahnee-eyaw.*
일부러 그러려고 했던 건
   아니야.

It was just a game.

geunyang jangnan chin
   geoya.
*geuh-nyahng jahng-nahn
   cheen guh-ya.*
그냥 장난친 거야.

**Stop playing these
   games.**

jangnan geuman hae.
jahng-nahn geumahn hay.
장난 그만해.

Stop nagging.

jansori jom geuman hae.
*jahnsoh-ree chohm geumahn
   hay.*
잔소리 좀 그만해.

We did it only once.

gyeou han beon bakke an
   haesseo.
*gyaw-oo hahn buhn bah-kkay
   ahn hess-uh.*
겨우 한 번 밖에 안 했어.

**Don't act like my
   husband!**

nae nampyeon / manura
   cheoreom gulji ma.
*nay nahm-pyawn / mah-noo-
   rah chuh-ruhm gooljee
   mah.*
내 남편 / 마누라 처럼
   굴지 마.

마누라 (**manura**) doesn't simply mean wife, but specifically an older, most likely nagging wife. The implication isn't just that of a wife, but of a wife to whom you've been married for a long time and who is used to being in charge around the house.

Don't act like I'm yours.	nal dangsin soyumul cheoreom chwigeup haji ma. *nahl dahngsheen soh-yoo-mool chuh-ruhm chwee-geup hahjee mah.* 날 당신 소유물처럼 취급하지 마.
Go look in the mirror!	geoul jom bosiji! *gaw-ool chohm bohshee-jee!* 거울 좀 보시지!
I've had it!	jigyeowo jukgesseo! / neondeoriga na! *jee-gyaw-wah jook-gess-aw! / nuhn-duh-ree-gah nah!* 지겨워 죽겠어! / 넌더리가 나!

These two options can be used interchangeably.

You mean nothing (to me).	dangsineun (nahante) amu geotdo aniya. *dahngsheen-eun (nah-hantay) ahmoo guhtdoh ahnee-ya.* 당신은 (나한테) 아무 것도 아니야.

I'm glad we broke up!

heeojyeoseo cheonman
dahaengiya!
*hay-uh-jyuh-saw chuhn-mahn
dah-hayng-ee-ya!*
헤어져서 천만다행이야!

(Pack your stuff and) hit the road!

(jim ssaseo) naga!
(jeem ssahsuh) nahgah!
(짐 싸서) 나가!

Give me back the apartment / car key.

apateu / cha ki dollyeo jwo.
*ahpahteuh / chah kee dohl-
lyaw jwah.*
아파트 / 차 키 돌려 줘.

Give me back all the presents I gave to you.

naega jwotdeon seonmul da
dollyeo jwo.
*nay-gah jwotduhn suhnmool
dah dohl-lyaw jwah.*
내가 줬던 선물 다 돌려 줘.

I've already thrown them away.

imi da beoryeosseo.
eemee dah buh-ryawssuh.
이미 다 버렸어.

Why'd you do such a thing?

wae geureon jiseul hae-
sseo?
way geuruhn jeeseul hess-uh?
왜 그런 짓을 했어?

(Because) I wanted to forget you.

dangsin ijeobeoriryeogu.
*dahngsheen ee-juh-buh-ree-
ryaw-goo.*
당신 잊어버리려구.

Don't do such a thing. geureon jit haji ma.
geu-ruhn jeet hahjee mah.
그런 짓 하지 마.

You're such a worrier. sosim hagineun.
soh-shim hah-gee-neun.
소심하기는.

You're such a crybaby. i ulboya.
ee ool-boh-yah.
이 울보야.

I'm not your toy. nan dangsine jangnangami
  aniya.
*nahn dahngsheen-ay jahng-
  nahn-gahm-ee ahnee-ya.*
난 당신의 장난감이
  아니야.

**Don't think that I'm
  only yours.** naega nikkeorago saenggak
  hajima.
*nay-gah nee-kkuh-rahgoh
  saynggahk hahjeemah.*
내가 니꺼라고
  생각하지마.

I don't belong to you. nan nikke anya.
nahn nee-kkay ahnyah.
난 니께 아냐.

Now I'll feel better (because we broke up).

(heeojinikkan) sogi da huryeon hane.
(hay-uh-jee-nee-kkahn) sohgee dah hoo-ryawn hahnay.
(헤어지니깐) 속이 다 후련하네.

You said bad things about me.

nae hyung bwatji.
nay hyoong bwaht-jee.
내 흉봤지.

How can you talk (to me) like that?

nahante eotteoke geureoke malhal su isseo?
nah-hahn-tay uh-tuh-kkay geu-ruh-kay mahlhahl soo eessuh?
나한테 어떻게 그렇게 말할 수 있어?

Crazy man!

michinnom!
mee-cheen-nom!
미친놈!

Bitch / Crazy woman!

michinnyeon!
mee-cheen-nyawn!
미친년!

You talk down to me.

dangsineun nareul musi haesseo.
dahngsheen-eun nahreul mooshee hess-uh.
당신은 나를 무시했어.

You talk to me like I'm a fool.

dangsineun nal babo
  chwigeup haesseo.
*dahngsheen-eun nahl bahboh
  chwi-geup hess-uh.*
당신은 날 바보취급했어.

(You have) no common sense.

gaenyeomeopda.
gay-nyawm-awp-dah.
개념없다.

개념 is derived from a Korean word meaning "notion," and is commonly used to mean "common sense." 없다 means "to not exist," so you can see why this would be offensive.

Who cares?

geureodeunga, maldeunga!
*geu-raw-deun-gah, mahl-
  deun-gah!*
그러든가, 말든가~!

I hate you!

na neo sileo!
nah naw shill-aw!
나 너 싫어!

You're childish!

eomsaljaengi!
awm-sahl-jaeng-ee!
엄살쟁이!

Whatever, stop talking.

dwetgeodeun!
dweht-goh-deun!
됐거든!

In other words, you're tired of hearing excuses. This literally means, "That'll do" or "That's enough."

I can find someone better than you.

neoboda deo gwaen-
    chaneun saram
    neollyeosseo.
*naw-boh-dah duh gwehn-
    chahn-eun sahrahm null-
    lyuss-aw.*
너보다 더 괜찮은 사람
    널렸어.

Who would want you?

nuga neogateun saram
    joahalkka?
*noogah naw-gah-teun
    sahrahm choh-ah-hahl-
    kkah?*
누가 너같은 사람
    좋아할까?

You're not the only boy / girl in the world.

namjaga / yeojaga neo
    hanan jul ala?
*nahmjah-gah / yaw-jah-gah
    naw hahnahn jool ahlah?*
남자가 / 여자가 너
    하난줄 알아?

The literal translation of this Korean expression is, "Do you think you're the only boy / girl?"

You can't find anyone better than me.

naboda deo gwaenchaneun
    saram chatgi him-
    deulgeol?
*nahbohdah duh gwehn-
    chahn-eun sahrahm
    chahtgee heem-deul-gull?*
나보다 더 괜찮은 사람
    찾기 힘들걸?

I can see whomever I want / do whatever I want.

jigeumdo mamman meogeumyeon dareun yeoja / namja eolmadeunji sagwil su isseo.

chig-eum-doh mahmmahn maw-geu-myuhn dah-reun yawjah / namjah ull-mah-deun-jee sah-gwil soo iss-uh.

지금도 맘만 먹으면 다른 여자 / 남자 얼마든지 사귈 수 있어.

Do it!

hae bwa!

hay bwah!

해봐!

Go find yourself a new boyfriend / girlfriend.

sae namchin / yeochin-ina cha-jabwa.

say nahmcheen / yawcheen-eenah chah-jah-bwah.

새 남친 / 여친 이나 찾아봐.

I've been lying to you / cheating on you.

na neohante geojinmal hae-wasseo. / na baram pyeo-sseo.

nah naw-hahn-tay guh-jeen-mahl hay-wahssaw. / nah bahrahm pyawssaw.

나 너한테 거짓말 해왔어. / 나 바람 폈어.

I don't want to believe that.

mitgo sipji anha.

meetgoh ship-jee ahnah.

믿고 싶지 않아.

Cheater! Two-timer!

baram dung-i! yang dari!

bahrahm doong-ee! yahng dahree!

바람둥이! 양다리!

I have another boyfriend / girlfriend.

dareun namchin / yeochin-i isseo.

dahreun nahmcheen / yawcheen-ee iss-aw.

다른 남친 / 여친이 있어.

I've tried to tell you many times, but I couldn't.

myeot beonina mal haryeogo haetneunde, mothaesseo.

myawt buhn-eenah mahl hah-ryaw-goh heht-neun-day, moht hess-aw.

몇 번이나 말하려고 했는데, 못했어.

I know you're seeing someone else.

jigeum baram pigo itneun geo ala.

chig-eum bahrahm peegoh een-neun guh ahlah.

지금 바람피고 있는 거 알아.

I saw you with another girl / guy.

dareun yeoja / namja rang gachi in-neun geo bwasseo.

dahreun yawjah / nahmjah rahng gah-chee een-neun guh bwahssaw.

다른 여자 / 남자랑 같이 있는거 봤어.

What kind of girl / guy is she / he?

gyae eotteon saramiya?

gyay aw-ttuhn sahrah-meeyah?

걔 어떤 사람이야?

I believed in you, yet you tricked me.

neol mideotneunde, neon nal sogyeosseo.

null mee-duhn-neun-day, nawn nahl soh-gyawssaw.

널 믿었는데, 넌 날 속였어.

Choose: her / him or me.

seontaek hae: gyaeya, naya?

suhntak hay: gyay-yah, nahyah?

선택해: 걔야, 나야?

Have you already decided (which one)?

gyeoljeong haesseo?

gyull-juhng hess-aw?

결정했어?

I won't forgive you.

neol yongseo haji aneul geoya.

null yongsuh hahjee ahneul goy-ah.

널 용서하지 않을거야.

Be nice to your new sweetheart.

sae aein hante jal hae.
say ay-een hahn-tay jahl hay.
새 애인한테 잘해.

Don't make her / him sad.

geu yeoja / namja seulpeuge haji ma.
geu yawjah / nahmjah seul-peu-gay hahjee mah.
그 여자 / 남자 슬프게 하지 마.

Don't make promises you can't keep.

jikiji mothal yaksogeun haji ma.
jeekeejee moht-hahl yahk-sohg-eun hahjee mah.
지키지 못할 약속은 하지 마.

I can't stand it.

chameul suga eopseo.
chahm-eul soogah up-saw.
참을 수가 없어.

You left without telling me.

neon maldo anhago ga beoryeosseo.
nawn mahldoh ahnnah-goh gah-buh-ryuss-aw.
넌 말도 안하고 가버렸어.

I can't give her / him up.

geu yeoja / namja pogiga an-dwae.
geu yawjah / nahmjah poh-geegah ahn-dway.
그 여자 / 남자 포기가 안돼.

I can't forget her / him.

geu yeoja / namja ichyeo
    jiji anha.
geu yawjah / nahmjah ee-
    juh-jee-jee ahnah.
그 여자 / 남자
    잊혀지지 않아.

I can't forgive her / him.

geu yeoja / namja
    yongseoga andwae.
geu yawjah / nahmjah yong-
    suh-gah ahn-dway.
그 여자 / 남자 용서가
    안돼.

12

Slang, Internet, and Other Useful Phrases

That's a killer!   juginda!
                          joogeenda!
                          죽인다~!

This is used when you're really satisfied with something. For example, it means "she / he is really hot!"

Do you wanna die?   jukgo sipeo?
                          jook-goh ship-paw?
                          죽고싶어?

Note: this is NOT an insult or meant seriously—just a way of reinforcing your point. Think about the way your mom used to say you'll freeze to death if you didn't wear your hat in the cold weather.

The next four expressions all mean "That's great!" and all originated with "the younger generation." While the first, 짱이다~!, is commonly used now even among older people, the other three are still used only by young people.

That's great!	**jjangida!**
	jjahng-eedah!
	짱이다~!
	jaksarida!
	jahk-sah-ree-dah!
	작살이다~!
	jidaeda!
	jeeday-dah!
	지대다~!
	daebakida!
	day-bahg-ee-dah!
	대박이다~!
Damn good!	**jolla jota!**
	chohl-lah chohta!
	졸라 좋다~!
roommate	**rumme**
	room-meh
	룸메
housemate	**hame**
	hah-meh
	하메
a person who has a good figure	**momjjang**
	mohm-jjahng
	몸짱
a person who is very handsome / beautiful	**eoljjang**
	ull-jjahng
	얼짱

a very adorable guy / girl

wansonam / wansonyeo
wahn-soh-nahm / wahn-soh-nyaw
완소남 / 완소녀

a friendly(-looking) man / girl

hunnam / hunnyeo
hoon-nahm / hoon-nyaw
훈남 / 훈녀

This phrase is often used even if the person is not necessarily traditionally handsome / pretty.

a curvy woman

jjok-jjok bbang-bbang taeng-taeng
jjok-jjok bbang-bbang taeng-taeng
쭉쭉빵빵탱탱

쭉쭉 means "tall," 빵빵 means "a large chest," and 탱탱 describes their butt. Pick and choose if you like.

a man / woman who has no job

baeksu / baekjo
becksoo / beck-joh
백수 / 백조

a man / woman who indulges in too much luxury

doenjangnam / doenjangnyeo
dwenjahng-nahm / dwenjahng-nyaw
된장남 / 된장녀

These are recently-coined words, and in popular use. If you wear only brand-name clothes, for example, and generally spend too much money, you may hear this term!

He / she sucks.
(gyae) bammasiya! /
(gyae) jaesu eopseo!
(gyay) bahm-mah-sheeyah! /
(gyay) jay-soo up-saw
(개) 밥맛이야~! /
(개) 재수없어~!

Here are two interchangeable options for conveying this. Notice that the word 개 indicates the "he / she" portion of the sentence. But remember that in Korean the subject of a sentence is usually omitted, which is why 개 is in parentheses: you can say it, or not. The second of these two expressions is much worse than the first. The first means "rice taste" and comes from young people who are sick of rice and prefer other options, so it basically means something / someone you're tired of seeing. The second literally means "no luck" (but don't use 재수 (**jaesu**) for luck in any other context). It means that the sight of someone is so unpleasant that it actually brings bad luck upon you. Pretty harsh.

He / she is a bomb!
gyae poktan-iya!
gyay pohk-tahn-eeyah!
개 폭탄이야~!

In Korean, this means that he / she is really ugly. They are *a* bomb, not *the* bomb.

Netizen
nurikkun
noo-ree-kkoon
누리꾼

The following phrases are all in polite speech, unlike the rest of this chapter.

Let me know your Facebook / Twitter.

peiseubuk / twitteo jusoreul jom gareuchyeo juseyo.
peh-ee-seu-book / twee-tuh joosoh-reul chohm gah-reu-chyaw joo-say-yo.
페이스북 / 튀터 주소를 좀 가르쳐 주세요.

Let me know your e-mail address.

i-meil jusoreul jom gareuchyeo juseyo.
ee-may-il joosoh-reul chohm gah-reu-chyaw joo-say-yo.
이메일 주소를 좀 가르쳐 주세요.

Let's go to an Internet café!

PC bahnge gallaeyo?
PC bahng-ay gah-lay-yo?
PC방에 갈래요?

A PC 방 is a Korean-style Internet café which mostly focuses on Internet use, rather than on café-style food or drinks.

Do you have a digital camera?

dika isseoyo?
deekah eessuh-yo?
디카 있어요?

This is a selfie.

sselka yeyo.
sselkah yeyo.
셀카예요.

Sselka is the meaning for "selfie".

Do you want to chat with me online?

chaeting hallaeyo?
chateeng hahl-lay-yo?
채팅할래요?

Do you want to video-chat with me online?	**hwasang chaeting hallaeyo?** *hwahsahng chateeng hahl-lay-yo?* 화상채팅할래요?

And now, back to slang. All the phrases below are, again, very informal.

It's shocking / touching / really funny.	**anseubida.** *ahn-seu-beedah.* 안습이다~!

The Korean literally means "My eyes are full of water (tears)." Which makes sense when you consider that your eyes become watery when you're shocked, touched, or laughing hilariously.

What a shame! / It's really embarrassing!	**a, jjok pallyeo!** *ah, jjohk pahl-lyaw!* 아, 쪽팔려~!

When you're at a loss, in a dilemma, or in an awkward position, you can say:

daeryak nangamine!
day-ryahk nahn-gahmee-nay!
대략 난감이네~!

When things / people around you make you angry or displeased, try out this commonly heard Korean phrase... but don't say it in polite society:

a, jjang na~!
ah, jjang nah~!
아, 짱나~!

When you're angry, you can also say one of these interchangeable phrases:

a~ yeol badeo!
ah yawl bahdaw!
아~ 열받어!

a~ yeol ppeotchyeo!
ah yawl ppuht-chuh!
아~ 열뻗쳐!

a~ ttukkeong yeollyeo!
ah ttoo-kkuhng yull-lyaw!
아~ 뚜껑 열려!

a~ kkokji dola!
ah kkohk-jee dohl-ah!
아~ 꼭지 돌아!

When you're shy, you can say:

bukkeu bukkeu.
bookkeu bookkeu.
부끄 부끄.

When the atmosphere is boring or someone's joke is not funny, you can say this (the meaning is the same, whether you say the 해 **hae** or not):

sseolleong (hae)!
ssull-luhng (hay)!
썰렁(해)!

When you see an embarrassing or shocking moment, you can say:

heogeok!
haw-guhk!
허걱~!

**I'm goofing around
(in my room).**

bangbadak geukgo isseoyo.
*bahng-bah-dahk geul-kkoh
    eessuh-yo.*
방바닥 긁고 있어요.

This handy phrase's literal meaning is, "I'm scratching my room's floor."

The word 방콕 (**bangkok**), as well as referring to the capital of Thailand, is also slang for "just hanging out in your room."

**What did you do all
weekend?**

jumale mwo haesseo?
joo-mahl-ay mwoh hess-aw?
주말에 뭐 했어?

**Oh, I just hung out
in my room.**

Ah, bangkokman haesseo.
*Ah, bahng-kohk-mahn
    hess-aw.*
아, 방콕만 했어.

**Speak of the devil,
then he'll appear.**

horangido je mal hamyeon
    natanandadeoni.
*haw-rahn-gee-doh jay mahl
    hahmyuhn nahtah-nahn-
    dah-duh-nee.*
호랑이도 제 말하면
    나타난다더니.

Instead of "devil," Koreans say "tiger." You can also briefly say just **Horangi**, meaning "tiger," for this phrase.